THE POWER

OF THE

PLATFORM

SPEAKERS ON PURPOSE

www.LVCSB.com
Las Vegas Convention Speakers Bureau

THE POWER OF THE PLATFORM
Speakers on Purpose

Published by TwoBirds Publishing, Inc.
and
Las Vegas Convention Speakers Bureau
www.LVCSB.com

2657 Windmill Pkwy, #116, Henderson, NV 89074

Copyright © 2009 TwoBirds Publishing, Inc.
Library of Congress Control Number: 2009933781
ISBN-13: 978-0-9754581-6-7

Cover Design by Julia Lauer with Ambush Graphics
Editing and Composition by
Robin Jay & Michelle Johnson
Pages formatted by Randi Ball
with Obsessive Formatting & Design

Special Note: This edition of "The Power of the Platform - Speakers on Purpose" is designed to provide information and motivation to our readers. It is sold with the understanding, that the publisher is not engaged to render any type of psychological, legal, or any other kind of professional advice. The content of each article is the sole expression and opinion of its author, and not necessarily that of the publisher. No warranties or guarantees are expressed or implied by the publisher's choice to include any of the content in this volume. Neither the publisher nor the individual author(s) shall be liable for any physical, psychological, emotional, financial, or commercial damages, including but not limited to special, incidental, consequential or other damages. Our view and rights are the same: You are responsible for your own choices, actions, and results.

Printed in the United States of America

10 9 8 7 6 5 4 3 2 1

ACKNOWLEDGEMENTS

When experts come together in an anthology, readers get a whole that is greater than the sum of its parts.

I want to express my deepest gratitude to those experts who gave of their time and wisdom to make this book extraordinary. Your generosity enables me to share your precious, life-altering messages with thousands of readers worldwide. Jack Canfield, Brian Tracy, Keith Ferrazzi, Marci Shimoff, Richard Bolles, and Les Brown – you are each in a league of your own. I am blessed to know you and am privileged to work with you. Thank you so much.

My warmest gratitude also goes out to my many coauthors. We've transcended 15-hour time zones, Skyped, e-mailed, and shared through all hours, day and night, to bring messages that will encourage, inspire, and inform. It has been a joy getting to know you and a blessing to work with you. Thank you.

Special thanks to my team, Michelle Johnson and Randi Ball, for being patient, kind, and caring. I count on you more than you realize.

Finally, I'm grateful for readers like you who aspire to understand more about life and to grow. You will soon discover answers to your most profound questions! I appreciate you deeply.

~ *Robin Jay*

FOREWORD

A speaker is someone who earns part or all *(though rarely "all")* of their living, from getting up in front of groups and speaking, usually at conventions or meetings. That's the long and the short of it. Beneath that generalization lies, however, a bewildering variety of possibilities.

Technically, a teacher of, say, "How to Use PowerPoint" is a speaker. Technically, a preacher is a speaker. So is the author of a book. So is an entertainer or celebrity. So is a pitchman, like the late Billy Mays. So is a politician, or an orator, skilled at moving or motivating listeners.

There are, not surprisingly, sub-species of speakers, such as "inspirational speakers" and "motivational speakers." Speakers may be old legendary names, such as Zig Ziglar. Or brand new names, such as whoever is the author of the latest popular bestseller.

But every speaker has a limited "shelf-life." *Fickle public, and all that.* Speakers are like a comet; while they are in view, popular and blazing a trail across the firmament, their work is intoxicating. To be able to motivate people, to move them to tears, to inspire them to action, well, is there anything more thrilling than that? Ask a speaker, in those years, if there is anything else they would rather do, and they will tell you, "No, no, no."

I have been a speaker, now, for more than forty years. I love it. I have spoken to groups as small as six and as large as ten thousand. I am still giving keynote addresses at conventions each year. *(Lucky me... long shelf-life!)* But, with all that experience there has been lots of time for reflection about various things, including why people buy books like this. I know that some of you have bought this book because your favorite speaker is included. Yes, and what a great collection this is! I like to listen to them, myself.

Here are some facts about those who strive to be the best speaker possible:

1. They never talk about anything unless they care deeply about it. There is no substitute for passion in speakers. If a speaker decides to give speeches only about subjects they think will "sell", but for which they have little feeling, everyone will know it. They don't keep giving the same "canned" speech, month after month, year after year. They would grow tired of it, and it will show. The

best speakers will tear up their old notes and create something fresh each time they speak. It keeps THEM creative, alive, and on fire.

2. Speaking, at its best, is truth coming through their personality. Both elements are necessary. If speeches are only filled with tons of stories about themselves, listeners will get their personality, but not their truth. On the other hand, if they keep their life entirely out of their speeches, listeners will get their truth, but not with any of the rich coloring that the speaker's personality would lend. Great speakers marry the two: what they care about, and who they have become as a result of that caring.

3. They don't delude themselves into thinking that they are the most important person in the room. The simplest child there may be greater than them, and they know that. When each fan comes up to a speaker afterward, great speakers treat them as if a king or queen were approaching them. They focus on them, ask them about their life, and listen hard. For, in the end, the best speakers are also the best listeners.

Dick Bolles, Author
What Color Is Your Parachute?
10 million copies sold
www.jobhuntersbible.com

TABLE OF CONTENTS

Introduction

A Story about Living a Life "On Purpose"

In 1985, my brother, Barry, bought me a gift of Dick Bolles' best-selling career guide, **What Color is Your Parachute?** In his book, Dick explained why traditional job searches fail and so many of us end up just working for a living until, twenty years later, we find ourselves with unrealized potential and broken dreams. He also shared how to avoid these pitfalls and realize our highest goals.

I took Dick's advice then, which led to nearly twenty incredibly successful, happy years in media sales. When I was ready for another dramatic change, I knew what to do. A few months ago, when I received an e-mail from Dick offering to help me with this book, I nearly fainted!

When you follow your purpose and passion, miracles happen!

I could not have imagined that twenty-five years after reading **What Color Is Your Parachute?**, I would receive an e-mail from the author offering to work with me.

When you are following your purpose and passion, living with the *intention* of achieving your dreams, the events of your life will start to amaze and astound you. Like magic, you will begin to attract all the right people into your life and start to enjoy the life you were meant to have.

It's hard to believe that many people don't even know that help is just a book away. Many of the speakers in this book also offer coaching, consulting, and programs to help you get from where you are to where you want to be.

Warmest wishes to you for a life filled with purpose and unbounded rewards.

~ *Robin Jay*

As the beloved originator of the ***Chicken Soup for the Soul®*** series, **Jack Canfield** watched the series grow to a billion dollar market. This alone makes him uniquely qualified to talk about success. He is also the author of the best-selling ***The Success Principles: How to Get from Where You Are to Where You Want to Be.***

Affectionately known as "America's #1 Success Coach," Jack is America's leading expert in creating peak performance for entrepreneurs, leaders, managers, sales professionals, employees and educators. Over the past 30 years he's helped hundreds of thousands of individuals achieve their dreams.

Jack is a Harvard graduate with a Master's Degree in psychological education and is one of the earliest champions of peak performance. He has a gift for sharing his methodology and results-oriented activities to help others produce breakthrough results. For more information on booking Jack for your next event, please visit:

Website: *www.JackCanfield.com*
E-mail: *Info4jack@jackcanfield.com*
Twitter: *@J_Canfield*
Facebook: *JackCanfieldFan*
Phone: *805-563-2935*

Chapter One

Making Your Life Work the Way You Want It To

Jack Canfield

We now live in a time of greater uncertainty and more unsettling economic news than recent years. These circumstances should compel us to take a deep breath, and pause to think about our lives.

When things happen in the world that seem so far beyond our individual control, it can feel unsettling. Don't give up on your goals and dreams just because "the time isn't good" You can choose to make ANY time the perfect time to uncover a whole new you! Even in tough times, you get to decide how to respond to certain conditions, opportunities, and outcomes—both good and bad.

Life will always be a series of choices and YOU get to decide on what will move you closer to your goals and your purpose, or farther away from them. External forces will always be part of the equation, even during the good times when the world is thriving.

When people ask me about the single most important ingredient to success, I always share the same response: realizing what's making you achieve success, and then realizing what is *stifling* your success.

Sometimes, recognizing the things that are NOT working in your life can be painful, yet VERY powerful to shaping the life you want. Don't try to rationalize them, make excuses for them, or hide them. This is when it's even more critical to take personal inventory and evict those excuses, rationalizations, and hidden habits that don't serve you. These things will keep you from the life you want to be living. Let me give you some examples. Ask yourself if you relate to any of these questions:

- **Do you want to be active, fit, and strong?** *Then you have to stop making excuses about your weight, diet choices, and lack of exercise.*

- **Do you want to be in a loving relationship based on friendship and respect?** *Then you have to stop rationalizing why you and your partner are not communicating well.*

- **Do you want to embrace Monday mornings and feel excited about going to work every day?** *Then you have to stop hiding your true passions and go after whatever it is you really want to be doing day in and day out.*

- **Do you want to lose the debt forever?** *Then you have to stop ignoring your spending habits and get real about a creating budget that will pull you out of debt and allow you to reach financial freedom.*

- **Do you want to feel more connected to the people in your life, such as your children, friends, and colleagues?** *Then you have to stop complaining about your poor relationships and figure out why you don't feel as connected as you'd like to be.*

These things can be painful to look at because the truth is that you have to do something about them in order to make your life work the way you want it to.

You'll have to say no to the second helping of dinner and the dessert to follow and go through the awkward stage of getting into shape... You'll have to confront your partner about the areas that need work... You'll have to get past fears about changing your job or professional path... You'll have to cut back on your spending and be frugal... You'll have to take a good hard look at your personal relationships and perhaps consider your own shortfalls and weaknesses in communicating your needs and concerns.

Plain and simple, you will have to do something uncomfortable.

Successful people don't waste time in denial (or complain or make excuses for that matter). They face situations like a warrior. They look for the warning signs, they find out why things aren't working, and they go about fixing them - even when fixing requires problem solving, hard work, risk, and a level of uncertainty.

It's okay to identify a problem even though you **haven't a clue** about how to go about solving it right away.

The first step is just recognizing the issue, and then having faith that you'll figure it out with careful attention to it. That's how successful people live—in constant focus on goals, on results, on problem solving, and on the actions that get them to where they want to be.

Following are three things to do constantly in pursuit of your goals and dreams, however big or small:

- **Awareness:** Keep your awareness on the feedback you are getting from life and decide to address the situations immediately. Don't bottle up feedback, cast it aside, and avoid it like you would a pile of dirty laundry or a stack of unopened bills. Life tells you things every day. Do this. Don't do that. Think about this. Try me. Forget that. We live in a world that seemingly encourages us to live on autopilot. Successful people fly manually every day and so should you. When those feedback signals come in, listen to them and use them in planning your next step.

- **Commitment:** Commit to finding out why things aren't working and learn what will fix them. Once you start the process it will be much easier to continue. Nothing fruitful stems from inaction.

- **Trust:** Trust that making changes to the situation will ultimately bring about the best results. Sure you might go through a bit of discomfort during the change, and you may incur some unlikely or unwanted outcomes but, in the end, you will triumph!

So are you ready to admit the things that just are not working out? Make a list of the things in your life that are working against your success and ask how the situation can be improved. Commit to tackling just **one** of those issues and be brave!

If you need help organizing those "things" in your life, try using the following list of categories. I recommend reflecting on each of the 7 areas and ask yourself, "What's not working here in each one?" and then brainstorm 3 potential solutions.

1. Financial Goals
2. Career/Business Goals
3. Free Time/Family Time
4. Health/Appearance Goals
5. Relationship Goals
6. Personal Growth
7. Making a Difference

Remember, by facing what is not working, you will discover how to make your life work the way you want it to!

Robin Sax is a former prosecutor for Los Angeles County specializing in child sexual assault cases. Today, she is an outspoken advocate fighting for victims and is a legal commentator for *Larry King Live, Nancy Grace, The Today Show,* and *The Early Show.* She also is a host on *Justice Interrupted Radio.*

Robin's books include *Predators and Child Molesters: What Every Parent Needs to Know to Keep Kids Safe, It Happens Every Day: Inside the World of a Sex Crimes D.A.,* and *The Complete Idiots Guide to the Criminal Justice System.* She lectures at the UCLA School of Law and is an adjunct professor at the California State School of Criminal Justice. Visit Robin at:

Website: *www.robinsax.com*
E-mail: *robin@robinsax.com*
LinkedIn: *Robin Sax*
Twitter: *@robinsax*
Facebook: *RobinSax*
Phone: *310-650-6494*

Chapter Two

Two Lives: One Mission

Robin Sax

Ok, I'll admit it. My kids think their mom has psychic powers. Why? Because their mom is a D.A. Follow me after I drop them off each morning and you'll understand why they tow the line – even when they don't want to.

From the kids' school, I head east to L.A.'s Criminal Court Building. As I drive, the landscape changes dramatically; Starbucks is replaced by bail bonds shops; billboards shift from English to Korean, to Spanish, to Japanese; people go from waiting at bus stops to being passed out at bus stops. During this ride, I think about how lucky I am that my kids have no concept of the world I am about to enter – assuming I get to court on time!

Different Worlds

Few people can wrap their minds around how a "West Side Mom" can go downtown, work in the trenches of the Los Angeles crime scene, and find parallels in these two worlds. My "co-madres" (other moms) in my personal life cannot picture my court life, and my colleagues cannot fathom the details of my private life. In each of my existences, however, I field complaints about the growing problems adults are having with kids.

To my amazement, I've found that there are more similarities between these "polar opposite" worlds than you might imagine. Peek into my kids' classrooms, you would find that my children go to school with the offspring of celebrities, agents, athletes, and other influential people, including a state senator, a football team owner, and some high-flyers from the Fortune Top 100.

People mistakenly assume that parenting these privileged kids is a lot easier than parenting your "ordinary" kid. Nothing could be farther than the truth. Regardless of lifestyle, kids tend to have the same types of problems – low self-image, family problems, academic pressures, and student rivalries, to name a few. Walk into my courtroom on any day and you will find that these identical themes come up in the children's cases I handle.

Mom as a Superhero?

Because I work so closely with kids, my own family is convinced that somehow I have super powers – night vision, surveillance skills, even a built-in lie detector – that allow me to see things and know things that other parents can't possibly see or know.

The fact is, I don't have any super powers or secret information. I love that my kids think I do. My powers come in the form of skills and techniques learned from living in the trenches of the real world of conflict and crime.

As Deputy District Attorney for Los Angeles County, it is my job to uncover the truth in some of the meanest and messiest of circumstances and somehow ensure that the right thing is done. In order to get to the truth, I investigate, and uncover facts and evidence. Sometimes I prosecute, argue, and convict. Sometimes I cut people a break, offering alternatives to jail or fines. Sometimes I simply wait for further developments. I live and thrive in a world of investigation, conflict, and resolution. My world is the world of discipline, and it affects people of all ages, from young to very old.

But as a parent, I am no different than you. We parents are charged with the job of seeking the truth and administrating justice in our homes every day. And, because we are parents, we live, breathe, and encounter conflict and seek resolutions everyday. These conflicts in the courthouse are called "cases." Similarly, a parent's caseload is filled with "incidents," and every incident is an opportunity to apply discipline effectively.

The Truth about Incidents

Let me share a universal truth about "incidents": each one has the potential to escalate into a crisis. As parents, one of our most important jobs is to figure out how to manage the "incident" so we don't end up with a crisis. How will we handle a fib, a squabble, a fight, a blow-up, or a more serious departure from acceptable conduct?

It's important for us parents to recognize that an incident forces everyone to re-evaluate rules, consequences, and disciplinary schemes. And since there are so many incidents on a daily basis, we have countless opportunities to regulate our kids' behavior and, ultimately, raise children who will make us proud.

I've often heard people say, "There should be classes on this stuff!" Unfortunately, there is no formal education that grants us a Ph.D. in parenting. This is an education we can only acquire by doing, experimenting, screwing up, talking to others, and learning from others' mistakes.

Skillful parenting is a rare commodity. You'll find that when you're suddenly the parent of a child, you are now qualified to enhance – or mess up – somebody else's life. Being a parent is the most important job anybody can ever have. And, because it is so important, it requires training to do it right.

When I became a lawyer, I had to undergo a ton of formal education. Then, to be a top-notch prosecutor, I needed years of training and experience under my belt. But there was more to mastering this job than learning the skills of the courtroom. Being a prosecutor required an understanding of the most basic aspects of human nature and learning from them.

Similarly, what you need to learn to succeed as a parent *can* be taught. Effective parenting is not a mystery or an innate ability. It's a skill that can be acquired. In fact, parenting skills are pretty basic. There is no real magic... just a lot of common sense.

As a prosecutor, I teach jurors how to make the "right" decision. I don't *tell* them who is guilty; I present evidence that *shows* them who is guilty. I use a time-honored method, and over the years, I've learned how to effectively present a case, structure an argument, anticipate objections and defenses, and finally, a way to lay the whole damn thing to rest.

Just watch Court TV. You'll see that the above method works every day in courtrooms across the country. (Well, at least it works most of the time. After all, there was O.J.)

No matter what people think about lawyers, many wish they had the skills to think like one. Few people will disagree that legal training can come in pretty handy at times, especially in the business world. Everyone can see the benefit of being able to read a contract, negotiate a deal, or protect an interest. Applying legal skills to the business world is a natural leap. But here, we're interested in applying those skills to the job of parenting.

Think about it. Much of childrearing is advocating and presenting a way of life, (in legal terms known as a "case theory"), that you want your child to adopt. Every day we negotiate and mediate in our homes with our kids, as they do with us. And sometimes, when an incident occurs, negotiation and mediation are not enough; a full-blown crisis erupts.

Not a day goes by when an incident doesn't creep into my own personal "family case docket." Here's a typical morning at my house:

"Hannah, did you brush your teeth?"

"Yes, Mommy, I did."

"That's funny, because the toothbrush is completely dry."

"Uh-oh."

"Jeremy, where did you go last night? Who were you with?"

"The movies."

"What was the movie about? Do you still have the ticket stubs?"

"No."

"Anything else you want to tell me?"

"No."

"Oh, because I was just on MYSPACE and I saw pictures of you with a bottle of beer in your hand"...

"Uh-oh."

"Why do I have to get up at 6:30 A.M.? I can make it to school on time if I get up at 7:00! I'm 17... old enough to get up on my own," Jason informs me.

"That's true, but you are also responsible for getting your brother to school on time."

"Test me, you'll see."

"Okay, we'll give it a shot."

It's now 7:20 a.m. and Jason isn't up yet.

"Uh-Oh."

As a mom to three kids ranging from ages five to seventeen, I am – to put it mildly – busy. I am busy with them and with my life and career. To ensure that our time together is quality time, I have become the quintessential multi-tasker. This means I have to prioritize everything in my life.

Let's face it; none of us has time to read a different how-to book that addresses each kid, each issue, and each new parenting concern that might arise. Both our kids' needs and our parental roles change as each child enters a new and different developmental stage. In order to manage everything that looms before me as a parent, I have chosen to adopt the common-sense advocacy skills I use in court in handling my own home front "incidents" and in approaching discipline for kids of all ages. Once I began realizing that my two lives have the same mission – helping children – I became both a better parent AND a better prosecutor.

21

Andy Ebon is *"The Wedding Marketing Authority,"* one of the foremost thought leaders in the wedding industry. As a coach and consultant, Andy takes industry business owners to marketing excellence. Andy has more than twenty-five years in the disc jockey entertainment industry and more than a decade in Internet marketing.

In 2007, Andy turned his focus to educating wedding professionals on how to market their businesses creatively and successfully, primarily by showing them how to use the Internet and social media to define themselves as experts in their field. His specialized knowledge has propelled him into an international spotlight in this niche market.

Andy uses his expertise to help entrepreneurs and business owners in all industries to improve their Internet marketing skills and understanding. Please visit Andy at:

Websites:	*www.AndyEbon.com*
	TheWeddingMarketingBlog.com
E-mail:	*AndyEbon@AndyEbon.com*
LinkedIn:	*andyebon*
Twitter:	*@andyebon*
Facebook:	*andyebon*
Phone:	*888-275-0922, 702-227-9926*

Chapter Three

Building a Focused Social Media Strategy

Andy Ebon

The constant drumbeat of the national media drives people to social media sites, including **MySpace, Facebook, LinkedIn, Plaxo, Twitter, Blogging**... and the list goes on and on. We are made to feel that we *have* to be there, simply because everyone else is. Utilizing social media as a marketing tool, however, is not that simple.

You can build a *focused* **social media strategy** and use the strengths of the leading social media software tools. This will also help you to achieve your business goals and do so with greater speed.

Strategy First, then Tactics

Too often, people confuse strategy with tactics. Your *strategy* should be **clearly stated goals,** such as: *To generate better brand awareness among your target audience, increase referrals, appointments, and sales* (preferably, by specified amounts and within a given time frame).

In marketing, *tactics* are your means and messages of communication: Advertising, public relations, social media, etc. One should always want to improve sales, but we must remember to always connect the dots, from awareness to sales.

Look Before You Leap

Before you launch a blog, spend a few months reading other blogs. Choose to follow blogs that are posted by your competition, are about your favorite hobby, and are of special interest to you in any other way. Notice the difference between those blogs that speak to you as the reader, and those that scream **"Me, me, me!"** Which do you enjoy reading more?

Opening a social media account is easy. The hard part is to hold back from posting anything. Fill out your profile and observe the activity. By waiting a while before posting, you'll be able to observe and understand the genre better.

- What do you find interesting?

- What's unnecessary?

- What is pure nonsense?

Don't Get Seduced By Numbers

"Followers" on Twitter, **"Friends"** on Facebook, and **"Connections"** on LinkedIn all measure outreach. However, for individual business people, (as opposed to mega-brands), the person with greatest number of Followers, Friends or

Connections doesn't win the lottery. What is important is the **quality** of your connections.

The Wedding Marketing Blog: The Launch

In the fall of 2006, I decided to change the focus of my business from website and e-mail marketing for hospitality industry clients to complete marketing for the wedding industry. I wanted to show those in the wedding industry how to market effectively.

To accomplish this transition, I built and maintained a blog that provided interesting, challenging and provocative marketing information for the wedding industry. My ultimate goals were to increase speaking engagements, build my consulting business, and develop wedding marketing materials for sale.

After studying blogs, books about blogs, and podcasts about blogs for months, I launched **TheWeddingMarketingBlog.com** in February 2007. It was a modest success. As the blog developed rhythm and style, however, more and more readers found it - through search engines, referrals, and a couple of emails to my contact database. Readers subscribed, posted comments, and contacted me directly.

The Value of a Single Reader

Trying to evaluate the aggregate of a blog is nearly impossible. What rules is the quality of your readers. Having even just a couple of significant readers can make everything worthwhile.

In a few short months, I started getting inquiries for speaking engagements and consulting. It became obvious, quickly, that *focusing on the reader* was having a positive impact.

Adding Social Media to the Mix

The blog readership built steadily through the summer of 2008. That's when I threw some gasoline on the fire in the form of online social media. The primary strategy was straightforward: All social media activity was designed to define myself as **"The Wedding Marketing Authority"** and elevate the readership of **TheWeddingMarketingBlog.com.**

The Starting Point: Linked In

LinkedIn is a business-oriented social networking site. It offers opportunities to connect with current contacts, reconnect with people you have lost track of, and seek introductions to people you would like to meet. It has prolific functions for giving and receiving recommendations. You can join special interest groups for your alma mater, your hobbies, your business interests, or any number of other commonalities.

I posted my business profile, a long form resume of "everything-you-ever-wanted-to-know-about-me." Then, I searched the **LinkedIn** database for people from my present and past business circles. I invited them to connect and they did.

Next, I explored **"Groups."** Linked In offers tremendous opportunities to connect based upon common interests... or groups. Soon, my profile sported logos for various **Groups** I had joined. I also felt it would be advantageous to start a group of my own. I created **Wedding Marketing.** I now have more than 1000 Wedding Marketing members who discuss common topics that are related to the industry. As I release products and services, I keep the group apprised, both as an audience of potential buyers and evangelists.

LinkedIn offers the opportunity to syndicate your published blog directly into the business profile. By doing that, I immediately increased blog readership, even though those readers were not measured on **TheWeddingMarketingBlog. com** directly.

Facebook: 250 Million Users and Growing

In mid-2008, **Facebook** had about 80 Million users. One year later, it had more than tripled in size. What started as a purely personal-social website had evolved into a platform that serves people both personally and professionally.

You can have a personal profile, a separate and distinct business profile, and a group (fan page) for your business. Businesses can also take out small space ads, targeted by demographic points to specific sets of **Facebook** users. For example: Brides could be targeted via certain profile elements, such as: "engaged," "25-34," "college educated," or by a local zip code.

Like **LinkedIn, Facebook** can automatically incorporate content from a blog. It is clear that blog posts are being read via my **Facebook** account, because readers post comments, regularly. Again, the execution should be: Join, invite people you know to be your friends, and then watch and read for a while. Resist the temptation to post anything beyond your profile too quickly.

The Facebook Status Line

Facebook asks, **"What's on your mind?** This is where people either get it right... or go into a ditch. No one cares if you're stuck in traffic or if you had a ham sandwich for lunch. If your goal is to enhance your business profile, then craft your updates with that in mind.

Twitter Rockets into the Public Consciousness

No other online social media tool appears to have garnered more news coverage than **Twitter.** It is an information-sharing platform in the form of a 160-character message. You can follow people on **Twitter**, and vice-versa, but it is not a double-opt in situation. Just because you follow Ashton **Kutcher** does not mean he will follow you back.

My business strategy has been quite specific: 95% of my followers – and those I follow – are wedding industry businesses... period. Sometimes, I will use my **Twitter updates,** or **"Tweets,"** to share a post from my blog. Other times, a tweet will promote wedding industry news from elsewhere on the web.

The Power of the ReTweet

The viral nature of **Twitter** is the "**ReTweet.**" If a person is particularly impressed by a message, they can elect to forward it to their **followers.** Spreading of a message by "retweeting" can increase the distribution of your message geo-metrically, as it has for me.

Quantifying the Results

All of these social media tactics, each in their own way, have contributed to the success of my strategy:

- **LinkedIn** has been a methodical way to connect and reconnect. It has resulted in speaking and consulting bookings, increased blog readership, and at last count, over 500 Wedding Marketing Group connections.

- **Facebook** activity has been both business and personal in nature. Through its clean format, I make pithy status updates that create awareness of what I'm doing. Most importantly, updates about speaking engagements beget inquiries about future speaking opportunities. I'm able to let people know I'm thinking about them, make them laugh, congratulate them, or wish them a happy birthday, and can choose to do it publicly or privately. The personal side, too, can be interesting to business friends. A photo of my dog, Ray Charles II, garnered a slew of comments.

- **Twitter** has been a surprise. In April and May, 2009, **TheWeddingMarketingBlog. com** posted its two best readership months. By June, it had more visitors than in April and May combined! The beat goes on. The blog success can be attributed to many factors, but the huge jump in numbers is clearly based on **ReTweets** from **Twitter.** Blog activities aside, direct connections from Twitter include new consulting clients and speaking opportunities.

Plan Your Strategy, Then Execute Relentlessly

There is one other major factor in the success of my strategy. That is **continuity.** If you start a blog, stick with it. Don't abandon it because you opened a **Facebook** account or signed up for **Twitter.**

The strength of **online social media** is a catalyst for your marketing success. Each choice you make adds a different element. Combined and consistent implementation, fueled by the development of a clear strategy to achieve your goals, will move you toward business goals at lightening speed.

Marci Shimoff is a leading expert on happiness, success, and the law of attraction. She is the author of the ***New York Times*** bestseller, ***Happy for No Reason: 7 Steps to Being Happy from the Inside Out,* now in 31 languages and the subject of a nationwide television** special.

Marci is a featured teacher in ***The Secret*** and is co-author of the ***Chicken Soup for the Woman's Soul*** series. Her eight books have sold more than 14 million copies. She's one of the bestselling female nonfiction authors of all time.

Marci's been a top-rated speaker and trainer for Fortune 500 companies and audiences worldwide for over 25 years. She holds an MBA from UCLA. She is dedicated to helping people live empowered, joy-filled lives. Please visit Marci at:

Website: www.HappyForNoReason.com
Email: info@happyfornoreason.com
LinkedIn: marcishimoff
Twitter: marci_shimoff
Facebook: marcishimoff
Phone: 415-789-1300

Chapter Four

Happiness First

Marci Shimoff

I was 41 years old, stretched out on a lounge chair by my pool and reflecting on my life. I had achieved all that I thought I needed to be happy.

You see when I was a child, I imagined there were five main things that would ensure me a happy life: a successful career, a loving husband, a comfortable home, a great body, and a wonderful circle of friends. After years of study, hard work, and a few "lucky breaks," I finally had them all. (Okay, so my body didn't quite look like Halle Berry's, but four out of five isn't bad!) You think I'd have been on the top of the world.

Surprisingly, I wasn't. I felt an emptiness inside that the outer successes of life couldn't fill. I was also afraid that if I lost any of those things, I might be miserable.

I was very familiar with being "happy because..." but it didn't bring me the deep and lasting happiness I wanted.

Sadly, I knew I wasn't alone in feeling this way. While happiness is the one thing that we all truly want, so few people really experience the deep and lasting fulfillment that feeds the soul.

Looking around, I saw that the happiest people I knew weren't the most successful, wealthy, healthy, or famous. From where I stood, there seemed to be no rhyme or reason to what made people happy. The obvious question became: *Could a person actually be happy for no reason?*

I had to find out.

So I threw myself into the study of happiness, delving into the research of positive psychology. I interviewed scores of scientists, as well as 100 unconditionally happy people.

What I found changed *my* life.

Living *From* Happiness Instead of *For* Happiness

One day, as I sat down to compile my findings, all the pieces of the puzzle fell into place. I had a simple, but profound "a-ha"—there's a *continuum* of happiness:

Unhappy	Happy for Bad Reason	Happy for Good Reason	Happy for No Reason
Depressed	*High from Unhealthy*	*Satisfaction from*	*Inner State of*
	Addictions	Healthy Experiences	Peace & Well-being
----------External----------			*Internal*

Unhappy: We all know what this means: life seems flat. Some of the signs are anxiety, fatigue, feeling blue or low – your "garden-variety" unhappiness. This isn't the same as clinical depression, which is characterized by deep despair and hopelessness that dramatically interferes with your ability to live a normal life, and for which professional help is absolutely necessary.

Happy for Bad Reason: When people are unhappy, they often try to make themselves feel better by indulging in addictions or behaviors such as drugs, alcohol, excessive sex, "retail therapy," compulsive gambling, over-eating, and too much television-watching, to name a few. This kind of "happiness" is hardly happiness at all. It is only a temporary way to numb or escape our *un*happiness through flooting experiences of pleasure.

Happy for Good Reason: This is what people usually mean by happiness: having good relationships with our family and friends, success in our careers, financial security, a nice house or car, or using our talents and strengths well. It's the pleasure we derive from having the healthy things that we want in our lives.

Don't get me wrong. I'm all for this kind of happiness! It's just that it's only half the story. Being Happy for Good Reason depends on the *external* conditions of our lives—if these conditions change or are lost, our happiness usually goes too. We are afraid the things we think we need to be happy may be slipping from our grasp.

Deep inside, I think we all know that life isn't meant to be about getting by, numbing our pain, or having everything "under control." True happiness doesn't come from merely collecting an assortment of happy experiences. At our core, we know there's something more than this.

There is; it's the next level on the happiness continuum – Happy for No Reason.

Happy for No Reason: This is true happiness – a state of peace and well-being that *isn't* dependent on external circumstances.

Happy for No Reason isn't elation, euphoria, mood spikes, or peak experiences that don't last. It isn't an emotion. In fact, when you are Happy for No Reason, you can have *any* emotion—including sadness, fear, anger, or hurt—but you still experience that underlying state of peace and well-being.

When you're Happy for No Reason, you don't need to manipulate the world around you to try to make yourself happy. You *bring* happiness to your outer experiences rather than trying to *extract* happiness from them.

This is a revolutionary concept. Most of us focus on being Happy for Good Reason, stringing together as many happy experiences as we can, like beads in a necklace, to create a happy life. We have to spend a lot of time and energy trying to find just the right beads so we can have a "happy necklace."

Being Happy for No Reason, in our necklace analogy, is like having a happy string. No matter what beads we put on our necklace—good, bad or indifferent—our inner experience, which is the string that runs through them all, is happy, creating a happy life.

Your Happiness Set Point
So, how do we get there? Science is showing the way. Researchers in the field of positive psychology have found that we each have a "happiness set-point," that determines our level of happiness. No matter what happens, whether it's something as exhilarating as winning the lottery or as challenging as a horrible accident, most people eventually return to their original happiness level. Like your weight set-point, which keeps the scale hovering around the same number, your happiness set-point will remain the same **unless you make a concerted effort to change it**.

The great news is that you can raise your happiness set-point. In the same way you'd crank up the thermostat to get comfortable on a chilly day, you actually have the power to reprogram your happiness set-point to a higher level of peace and well-being.

The secret lies in practicing the habits of happiness. In fact, I identified 21 core happiness habits that anyone can practice to be happier. Here are three powerful happiness habits:

Believe That This is a Friendly Universe

One of the main habits that happy people share is believing that the universe is out to support them – that this is a friendly universe. When things don't seem to be going their way, instead of feeling like victims, they look for the lesson and the gift in the situation. In other words, they believe there is a higher purpose that is supporting their ultimate good.

Practicing this one habit has made a huge difference in my own life. Try it yourself: the next time you face a challenge, take a moment to reflect silently, asking yourself, "If this were happening for a higher purpose, what would it be?" I'm certain that whatever answer you discover will be illuminating, but, more importantly, you'll be tapping into that state of inner peace and well-being on a regular basis.

Savor the Good

Have you noticed that your mind tends to register the negative events in your life more than the positive? If you get ten compliments in a day and one criticism, what do you remember? For most people, it's the criticism. Scientists call this our "negativity bias" – our primitive survival wiring that causes us to pay more attention to the negative than the positive. To reverse this bias, get into the daily habit of consciously registering the positive around you: the sun on your skin, the taste of a favorite food, a smile or kind word from a co-worker or friend. Once you notice something positive that makes you feel good, take a moment to savor it deeply and *feel* it; make it more than just a mental observation. Spend twenty seconds soaking up the happiness you feel.

Make Your Cells Happy.
Your brain contains a veritable pharmacopeia of natural happiness-enhancing neurochemicals – endorphins, serotonin, oxytocin, and dopamine – just waiting to be released to every organ and cell in your body. The way that you eat, move, rest, and even your facial expression can shift the balance of your body's feel-good-chemicals, or "Joy Juice," in your favor. To dispense some extra Joy Juice—smile. Scientists have discovered that smiling decreases stress hormones and boosts happiness chemicals, which increase the body's T-cells, reduce pain, and enhance relaxation. You may not feel like it, but smiling—even artificially to begin with—starts the ball rolling and will turn into a real smile in short order.

The Fringe Benefits of Happiness
While success isn't the key to happiness, happiness is the key to success. Happy people naturally have greater opportunities, better health, deeper friendships, more customers and so on—plus they make more money. Research shows that people who are happy earn over $750,000 more in their lifetime than others.

But these benefits are just the icing on the cake, because being happy is its own reward. When you're Happy for No Reason, it's not that your life always looks perfect—it's just that however it looks, you are still happy.

Les Brown is the leading authority on releasing human potential and enhancing lives. A renowned professional speaker, personal development coach, author and television personality, Les has risen to international prominence by capturing audiences with electrifying speeches... challenging audiences to live up to their greatness.

Les is the recipient of the National Speakers Association's highest honor and has been selected as one of the **World's Top Five Speakers** by Toastmasters International. Les trains others to become better communicators and speakers as well, currently working with more than 3500 clients. His network enables all people to learn how to inspire others to new levels of achievement.

Les Brown is a master speaker who continues to reinvent himself to positively change the world. Visit Les at:

Website: www.LesBrown.com
Email: customerservice@lesbrown.com
Phone: 800-733-4226

Chapter Five

Your Power Voice

Les Brown

Discover Your Power Voice and Join the Ranks of the World's Most Effective and Persuasive Communicators

Your success hinges on how effectively you lead, empower, and inspire people to pour the best of themselves into the achievement of goals to serve humankind. Yet, to compete in today's uncertain times, we are faced with a new set of challenges. Now, you must do more...AND do it faster and better, with fewer resources and less manpower. So, how do you lead yourself and others through such jagged terrain while achieving higher levels of performance at the same time? The answer lies in your "Power Voice."

Your every-day *conversational voice* delivers information, facts, and data from your mind to the minds of your listener. Alternatively, your Power Voice is the expression of feeling and emotion that speaks from your heart to the hearts of others. It is commonly referred to as "heart-to-heart communication." But make no mistake; your Power Voice is much more than the colloquialism indicates.

Your conversational voice is sufficient for simple communication such as delegating a task, setting an appointment, or telling your spouse about your day. But when you need to make an impact and encourage people to take action – to buy from you, or to believe in an idea – a mere exchange of information isn't enough.

For instance, when you're selling an idea to members of the board, negotiating a deal, or uniting a team of employees, you need to back up what you say with the most powerful element that defines us as human. Your voice must carry *emotion.* Only your heartfelt emotions can reach the hearts of others to stimulate *their* emotions. And therein lies the master key to empower and influence the passions, beliefs, and even behavior of others. That's using your Power Voice.

Standard Equipment

As sure as you have feelings and emotions, you were born with the ability to communicate with them. Therefore, you, (like everyone), have always possessed a Power Voice of your own.

In a nutshell, your Power Voice is an inborn skill you can use to transcend virtually any obstacle to become more, do more, and have more than ever before, regardless of outside factors such as the economy, interest rates, inflation, and so on. But like any muscle in your body, its strength and power can only be developed with use.

When you discover your Power Voice, and learn specific methods for using it to capture attention, stimulate belief, and direct behavior, you access peak levels of efficiency and leverage, which translate into greater performance and achievement.

Unleashing Your Power Voice

To develop your Power Voice, there are two primary areas of emphasis:

The first is the **Messenger** – you, the person behind the words. This is where you analyze and develop your character, personality, self-confidence, and ability to communicate in a variety of situations. You tap into your ability to fully express yourself in every dimension of your life. Through the telling of your story, you create value your audience can grab onto and take with them long after they're out of your presence.

By developing the messenger in you, you can quickly and easily build your confidence, create committed listening from others, increase your selling abilities, and more.

The second area is the **Message** – what you say and how you say it. In creating your message, you mesh what you want to say with the outcome you want to achieve. And of course, you must also consider whom you are speaking to and in what setting. Are you closing a deal with a prospective client...and are you on their turf or yours? Are you looking to win the opinion of a business associate over lunch? Or are you speaking to a large group? These are some of the kinds of questions you must answer in preparation for delivering your Power Voice so it is well received and sure to win the hearts of your audience.

When you develop both the messenger and the message, your communications go beyond making a point. You maximize your connection with others while you bring out the best in them.

There are various ways to engage your Power Voice, depending on your audience, the circumstances, and your objective. As a leader, you are frequently required to empower teams to develop a larger vision of themselves, and to infuse their hearts and minds with the belief that they can achieve more than they thought they could. Once those things are in place, you can then motivate the team to act on these new beliefs in order to reach your goal.

Strategy: The Distract-Dispute-Empower Method

1. **Distract.** Whether your audience consists of 10 people or 10,000, each listener is connected with the story in their own head. It's your job to distract them from their own internal dialog and enroll them into committed listening. How? Through your message and the strategic delivery of your story, you can effectively engage their attention. Rather than speaking to segments of the audience, unite their thoughts and impact the total audience.

2. *Dispute.* As a leader, you are continuously working to challenge the existing beliefs that your audience has embraced. To provide them this hand up, your message needs to dispute their existing beliefs and offer alternative paradigms. To grab onto a new belief, they must let go of the other.

3. *Empower.* If steps one and two create the fertile ground, step three nurtures the seeds. Here, you inspire your audience to live beyond their mental conditioning and circumstances. You empower them to write new chapters in their lives. As a result everyone grows and achieves more.

People do not necessarily do what they're told, nor do they fully apply everything they're taught intellectually. People experience the greatest change and growth by ***doing.*** The value is in the *application* of knowledge.

Developing your Power Voice is no exception. It requires immersion, direct experience, practice, and guidance. Once you've experienced it, you heighten your ability to continuously grow and expand your leadership potential, which lead to having a greater impact on your career and your community.

Where your conversational voice may have only allowed you to communicate facts, figures, and information, your Power Voice literally inches those to whom you are speaking to the edge of seats. And with continued application, it will become your universal calling card that gives you access to unknown possibilities and experiences in life you have never imagined.

Robbie Chaney is an experienced educator who successfully transformed her teaching skills into effective tools for coaching adults. Her ability to train others comes from her formal education, which includes an undergraduate degree in Education and a Masters degree in Communications, Training, & Development, though she draws upon her practical life skills to motivate, empower, and entertain everyone she encounters.

Robbie has triumphed though devastating hardships and emerged with a burning desire to provide leadership to those who cannot see through the challenges set before them. She instills new hope in those who have lost touch with their life purpose due to hard times and adversity.

A successful business owner with a diverse background, Robbie thrives on helping others to define their core purpose in life. Visit Robbie at:

Website: www.ChaneyCoaching.com
E-mail: Robbie@ChaneyCoaching.com
LinkedIn: robbiechaney
Twitter: @robbiechaney
Facebook: robbiechaney
Phone: 314-921-8868

Chapter Six

Purpose through Faith

Robbie Chaney

In December of 1999, life was great. I was a happily married, stay-at-home mom with three small children – under five years old - living in an upscale community. My husband was a successful regional manager for GE, ex-military, a praise and worship leader, and known all around for his infectious laugh and smile. He had gone to the doctor for what he thought was allergies. Three weeks later he called me from the emergency room, where he had stopped on his way home from work, and said, "Robbie, the doctors found a tumor on my lung." I will always remember that day... how chilling and gut-wrenching it was... yet, somehow, I knew everything would work out.

He was diagnosed with a rare form of cancer know as lymphoblastic lymphoma, a very rare form of non-Hodgkin lymphoma in adults; it accounts for less than 3 in every 100 lymphoma cases overall. We fought, we prayed, and somehow we kept the faith through the trials and tribulations of this hideous disease. In just six short months, Jeffrey Flowers exited this life on earth and moved into that glorious life in heaven. Completely devastated, I was left to pick up the pieces. At the tender age of thirty-two, alone with three small children, I raised my fist up to God and questioned him, "NOW what?"

My faith helped me get through this incredibly challenging time. I knew I had to find my purpose. Somehow, I found the will to succeed; my faith was strong. It wasn't long before God restored my life; I got remarried and discovered my new purpose. Today, I find myself armed with the experience that helps me to coach others to succeed through life's most difficult blows.

If you've ever wondered what YOUR unique calling might be, get very quiet and listen. You will hear your heart telling you that you were put here on Earth to do something very special... and your heart will tell you exactly what that is.

Young or old, time is on your side. God's plan is amazing and He has gifted you with PURPOSE. I know you are searching for your own unique purpose. Perhaps you have already discovered it, but you are looking for ways to make it a reality. We are each provided the time and vision to achieve our own, unique purpose.

The first key to understanding your purpose is to **recognize it**! Have you ever felt a tugging at your heart? Has it changed throughout your life? When we are younger, we may feel a calling to create a family. As we get older, our vision may become more worldly or work-related. Throughout our lives as a whole, we usually feel the need to experience love, to share our lives with each other, and to accomplish something significant. It doesn't matter if you're twenty, sixty, or ninety years young - we all feel the urge to make a difference in some way, and to leave our mark on the world in which we live.

Getting Unstuck

Many people feel stuck, trapped in their present lives, or believe it's too late to pursue their dreams. My friend, don't believe this! You are carrying a dream by the very thoughts you keep and the words you speak! Focus on the possibilities and watch a miracle happen in your life.

Most of us struggle with the task of trying to find our purpose. Pastor Rick Warren's book, "The Purpose-driven Life" has sold more than **TWENTY-TWO MILLION** copies! People want answers! We think, "Wouldn't it be great if someone would just TELL US what we are supposed to be doing with our precious lives?"

I can't tell you what your specific purpose is, but I can help you discover it for yourself. Start by creating a blueprint for your vision. Keep in mind that your dream – or building – may be "under construction" for some time until you perfect it.

Trust in your ability to do whatever it is you were born to do. Your gift and what you do with it is your responsibility. When you discover your dream, you will encounter your ability.

This is such an incredible gift and you'll know it when it happens. I knew – without a doubt – that my purpose was to become a mentor by how I felt the first time I helped someone else achieve their dream.

Discipline is Vital to Success

Discipline yourself to stay focused on the possibilities – not the drawbacks. The possibility of accomplishing your dreams will be revealed when you decide to set your mind to go with your heart. Indian political and spiritual leader Mahatma Gandhi *(1869 – 1948),* said, *"Be the change you want to see in the world. To truly lead and make a difference in the world, you must always start with yourself."*

A successful person understands discipline. Discipline requires focusing on the end result. Many people have desires - they want to do this and they want to do that - but they don't have the discipline to adhere to the principles that will carry them to success. If your desire is to lose weight, but you don't have the discipline to eat healthy and exercise, you probably won't get the desired results.

The problem is that people fall short because they don't know what their desired end result IS! Once you know what success **means to you,** it will be easier for you to focus on the end result and, therefore, succeed.

Take Action!

Dreams are given to us through our imagination to inspire us and help us move forward... away from our current situation. Position yourself so that you can move forward when the time is right and your purpose is revealed to you. Write down your ideas, gifts, and talents and read them over every morning for a week. Then ask yourself, "Are these ideas truly a reflection of who I want to become?" If the answer is yes, then look at them often; focus on those ideas until they transform into concrete goals, helping you to visualize and move towards your purpose for your life.

When you grasp and understand what you were born to accomplish, that is purpose. When you can see your purpose with your mind by faith, and imagine it, that is vision. Vision demands change and taking action towards solving a problem. You were born to do something in life that leaves seeds for the next generation to take root and grow. Your vision should always inspire and help others. Take action!

Can You?

Embrace an attitude of *"Yes I Can!"* Every successful person will tell you the importance of writing down your goals. This is critical to your success because it directs your focus toward the desired result. Develop a plan and write it down. Be confident that God will reveal to you how to accomplish your vision. Only YOU are equipped to do exactly what you were called to do. Have confidence in who you are and know that you are perfect for your purpose.

Stay committed to fulfilling what you were born to do. Have an iron will, be persistent, and stick to it. Have a fierce, "bull dog" determination. A person with an iron will has staying power - the power to hold on. This determination will bring you strength and courage.

The 6th U.S. President, John Quincy Adams *(1767-1848)*, said, *"Patience and perseverance have a magical effect before which difficulties disappear and obstacles vanish."* Persistence is what makes the impossible possible. Think about it; there is nothing that can take the place of persistence and will power! Having determination means nothing can stop you - not hurt, pain, situations, criticism, family, dog, cat... nothing can stop you from crossing the finish line and gaining the prize!

When you're struggling to find these answers, know that your gift will make a way for you in the world and allow you to fulfill your vision. Ask the universe to reveal it to you. The Bible reads, "Ask God whatsoever things you desire when you pray; believe and you will receive them, and you shall have them." Have faith when you pray, believe God hears you, and believe that God will answer your prayers. Focusing on the questions in your mind and in your heart will help to bring about answers. Trust and have faith in this.

Don't miss your opportunity! Everyone is free to choose their destiny, their passion, and their purpose. Our life is the result of those choices.

It is my desire that you become highly motivated and that you find yourself eager to participate in the race toward your dream... armed with the passion necessary for you to achieve your goal. I want you to accomplish your greatest desires in God's purpose for your life. Lastly, I want you to soar toward your dream with strength and power. As you enjoy the journey, keep this in mind: the strength of your desire will determine the scope of your possibilities. You will recognize and experience yourself as a creative source. You will discover that the world has become a place of unlimited opportunities.

Chuck Bolton is a "C-level" executive coach, retained by CEOs and senior executives who seek positive change in their leaders and top teams through behavioral coaching. He is the developer of *Top Team Check*, a proprietary team assessment tool and has assessed more than 80 top teams in the U.S., Canada, Europe, and Israel.

Chuck is the author of *Leadership Wipeout: The Story of an Executive's Crash and Rescue* and *The Dirtiest Little Secret in Business: The Absence of Supportive Candor*.

Chuck speaks on leadership topics for corporations, associations, universities, and non-profits. He has appeared as an expert source in the national media, including CBS, NBC and FOX. For more information, visit Chuck at:

Website: www.chuckbolton.info
E-mail: Chuck@TheBoltonGroup.com
LinkedIn: ChuckBolton
Twitter: @ChuckBolton
Facebook: chuckbolton
Phone: 800-310-9020

Chapter Seven

The Dirtiest Little Secret in Business: The Absence of Supportive Candor

Chuck Bolton

There is an epidemic infecting many organizations small and large, from the CEO to front-line employees. It's a silent, contagious killer that destroys motivation and sucks out energy. It's the topic that everyone knows about, but no one acknowledges. It's the dirtiest little secret in business: a lack of supportive candor. Individuals and organizations need candor like the body needs oxygen, but all too frequently, people fail to express their true thoughts, share critical insights, or ask the tough questions on topics that are vital to the success of the business.

A lack of candor inhibits meaningful dialogue, which is essential for building strong, trusting relationships and improving business performance. The problem is more widespread than you may think. According to consulting firm *Leadership IQ*, nine out of ten people avoid giving constructive feedback to coworkers because they think it isn't worth it and they're afraid of the reaction. Also, according to a 2006 *Mercer Managemont Consulting* study, only forty percent of employees trust that their bosses communicate honestly.

Consider these examples:

Prior to the U.S. government bailout in 2008, did the "Big Three" U.S. auto makers face the real truth about the state of their business, the changing preferences of customers, their excess capacity, or their uncompetitive cost structure?

In 2007 and 2008, did the executive teams and Boards of Directors at AIG, Lehman Brothers, Washington Mutual, and Countrywide raise the tough questions about the health and sustainable performance of their businesses? Did they ask for the candid truth about their wild bets, the subprime mortgage balloon which was bound to burst, their institutions' liquidity levels and the likely impact of a "worst case" scenario?

For many of us, the examples we experience daily may be less dramatic, but they are significant nonetheless. Anyone can increase their ability to engage in supportive candor by learning how to effectively raise and manage conflict.

Supportive candor occurs when we *courageously* and *constructively* raise and discuss topics of importance to ourselves and others, when we give and receive *ongoing feedback*, and when we *collegially collaborate* to reach a better solution. When we are supportively candid, we speak our truth, learn the truth of others, and collaboratively create a shared truth. When we speak both candidly and supportively, the quality of our dialogue improves dramatically, engagement increases, relationships strengthen, decision-making improves, and teams function at a higher level. We also protect the sustainability of our companies and the interests of other stakeholders.

What Drives the Fear?

Why do we avoid being candid? Fear. We're afraid for a variety of reasons - losing our job or our stature, making a mistake, hurting someone's feelings, being rejected, causing anger, or being disliked. To be more supportively candid, we need to shift our perspective on how we view conflict. Rather than avoid conflict, create conditions so that we can safely discuss our perspectives and views thoughtfully, without allowing the discussions to deteriorate into disputes or hurt feelings.

Conflict can be constructive and instructive, or it can be destructive. Conflict is constructive and instructive when a greater diversity of ideas and decisions emerges to solve problems and exploit opportunities. Conflict can help mobilize teams to action, getting people engaged and aligned to focus on the task at hand. And the *process* of constructive conflict can lift the capabilities of individuals and teams, actually adding a richness and depth to relationships.

Conflict becomes destructive when issues become personal or when differences polarize individuals and groups, and when disputes are allowed to fester. Conflict becomes destructive when winning an argument becomes more important to us than choosing what is right. Commitment and energy can be sucked out of people when conflicts are poorly managed or when they become personal.

There are two forms of conflict: **Task-oriented conflict** is the normal, run-of-the-mill conflict that naturally occurs when people deal with issues, ideas, and approaches. **Acute conflict** occurs when issues deteriorate into ongoing, destructive, personal disputes. Task-oriented conflict can disintegrate into acute conflict if we don't manage the conflict process well.

How we respond to conflict is a choice we can handle many ways: we can bully others, play the victim, check out mentally or emotionally... we can even become passive-aggressive. Or, we can change our position and find agreement with the other party. We can engage in open discussion, using supportive candor to address the specific issue.

Clearly, engaging others is the most productive option for responding to conflict. To effectively engage, we need to have the right mindset and skill set to achieve excellent results. These include:

Being self-aware. Our thoughts drive our feelings and behaviors. Before being candid, we need to understand our own needs, motivations, and intent. Before we raise a sensitive topic with another individual or group, we need to consider: "What is the right thing to do? What are my *real* objectives? Am I sharing this perspective to help this person because I really care about them becoming their best, or am I sharing it just to help myself?"

Choosing love over fear. There are two basic human emotions: love and fear. Love is about positive intent, possibilities, and operating from a position of genuine concern, respect, encouragement, and support. Love is also courageous and honors "what is right." Love comes from the spirit whereas fear comes from the ego. Fear focuses on scarcity, anger, blame, cynicism, and guilt. Fear is where all negativity stems from.

When we lead with love, fear recedes. To effectively address conflict and create greater candor, ask yourself, "Am I operating from a love or fear-based perspective?" If it's a fear-based perspective, you can turn it around with your thoughts by doing an emotional and mental pivot. Think another thought. Addressing issues from a love-based perspective helps to achieve a productive outcome while being supportively candid.

Creating a safe place. When we speak with supportive candor - providing and seeking feedback - we create a safe place to exchange information and perceptions. Having a cup of coffee in a neutral setting or going for a walk provides a safer place than your office.

Reverent listening. Most of us seek to be heard and understood, but we don't really listen. Reverent listening is alertness to what is and isn't being said. It's listening as if the information you are hearing is the most important information in the world. When we listen to one another deeply and reverently, many conflicts are easily resolved.

Being empathetic. Fully put yourself in the shoes of the other person. Repeat what you have heard and paraphrase what the other person must be feeling. Doing so shows deep respect for the other person and their position.

Utilize self-communication skills. When we are able to ask clarifying questions and express our own needs and truths, we become more willing and able to collaborate to create positive solutions and new shared truths.

Leaders create the climate for supportive candor. The best leaders seek honest communication. They understand that candor and transparency are fundamental to creating cultures of collaboration and open communication, and support it as such. Leaders need to seek diverse points of view and invite others to share their perspectives and ideas.

This doesn't have to start with the CEO. It can start with each of us. Here are some suggestions to help you create a climate for supportive candor in your organization:

1. Ensure that goals and priorities are clearly and consistently communicated to all.

2. Take the time to align roles, responsibilities, and expectations; it's surprising how often a lack of clarity in these areas creates destructive conflict.

3. Be explicit in communicating your company's values as well as the norms of

acceptable behavior that you expect your team to display. Are the stated values and demonstrated values the same?

4. Encourage the members of your team to build strong relationships and to share clear, mutual expectations.

5. Identify problems quickly, before they have a chance to decompose. If there are taboo topics or "rotting fish" within your area of responsibility that need to be discussed, identify them and encourage your people to deal with them openly. Challenging as it may be, dealing with them is better than letting them fester.

6. Hold monthly one-on-ones with the members of your team to discuss their performance. Invite them to share their views regarding their own performance with regard to meeting their customer's needs as well as the needs of their peers, the people under them, and even their boss – YOU!

7. Regularly ask for feedback from your team members on how you are performing.

Leaders who best demonstrate supportive candor and show others how to do so recognize that each of us share similar needs. We all seek to have our voices heard. We seek recognition for being special and we want to feel that we are integral, and important to the team and company. Being mindful of these needs and other considerations will help you to develop an environment of supportive candor and a resonant working climate.

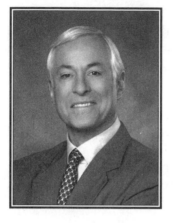

Brian Tracy has started, built, managed or turned around twenty-two businesses and has consulted for more than 1,000 businesses worldwide. He is president of Brian Tracy University of Sales and Entrepreneurship, a private, online college for business and entrepreneurship. He is also chairman and CEO of Brian Tracy International, a company specializing in the training and development of individuals and organizations.

He has written more than forty books on personal and business success that have been translated into thirty-four languages. He has written and produced more than 300 audio and video learning programs.

Brian speaks on the subjects of personal and professional development to corporate and public audiences, including the executives and staffs of many of America's largest corporations. His exciting talks and seminars on leadership, selling, self-esteem, goals, strategy, creativity and success psychology bring about immediate changes and long-term results. For more information, please visit:

Website: www.BrianTracy.com
E-mail: vrisling@BrianTracy.com

Chapter Eight

Planning for Success

Brian Tracy

There is a rule that "before you do anything, you have to do something else first." The first thing you have to do in business is to plan, and plan again, and keep planning until your plans work consistently to get you the results you want. The major reason for business failure is, first, failure to plan in advance and, second, failure to revise your plans if they do not work for some reason. Failing to plan is planning to fail.

What is the highest-paid work in business? Answer: *Thinking!* Thinking is the highest-paid work because of a special factor called "consequences."

You can always determine how valuable and important something is by measuring the potential consequences of doing it or not doing it. The potential consequences of having a cup of coffee or chatting with a coworker are virtually zero. It does not matter at all whether you do them or not. But the consequences of planning, of thinking through your actions before you begin, can be enormous. They can make all the difference between success and failure, poverty and wealth, happiness and unhappiness, a life of affluence or a life of despair.

Everything you are or ever will be is the result of your choices and decisions. Your choices and decisions have brought you to where you are today. If you are not happy about your current situation, then you must make new choices and better decisions for the future. There is no other way. And thinking is the essential ingredient in both choices and decision-making.

Start with Your Goals

In planning for success, you always start with yourself and your personal goals. Remember: your work and business life are means to an end. They are the things that you do so that you can enjoy the most important parts of your life – your family and your relationships.

Fully, 85 percent of your happiness in life will come from your relationships with other people. The greater clarity you have about what is really important to you, the better decisions you will make in both your business and personal life.

Remember the great question: "What do I really want to do with my life?" If you could wave a magic wand and be, do, or have anything at all in life, what would you choose for yourself? If you had all the time and money, all the friends and contacts, all the knowledge and experience, and no limitations at all, what would you really want to do with your life? This is the true beginning of personal strategic planning.

The 20/10 Exercise

Use the "20/10 Exercise." Imagine that you received $20 million cash in the bank today, tax-free. But simultaneously, you learned that you only had ten years left to live. If these two events happened simultaneously, $20 million cash plus only ten years to live, what would you choose to do with the rest of your life?

Who would you want to be with Who would you no longer want to be with? What would you want to do? Where would you want to go? What would you like to accomplish? What sort of legacy would you want to leave? These are some of the great questions of life.

Practice the Quick List Method

In our Focal Point Advanced Coaching and Mentoring Program, we put our clients through a "Quick List" exercise where we require them to write down three answers in less than thirty seconds to each of the following questions. Jot down answers for yourself.

1. What are your three most important overall goals in life, right now?

2. What are your three most important family or relationship goals, right now?

3. What are your three most important business goals, right now?

4. What are your three most important financial goals, right now?

5. What are your three most important health goals, right now?

6. What are your three most important community and social goals right now?

When you only have thirty seconds to write the answers to these questions, your answers will be as accurate as if you had thirty minutes or three hours. The answers that jump out at you with this 30-second exercise will usually be disturbingly accurate and will tell you immediately what is really important to you in each key area of life.

Your Major Definite Purpose

Here is a great question: "What one goal would you set for yourself if you knew you could not fail?"

Imagine that you could achieve any one goal, small or large, short term or long term. Imagine that you were absolutely guaranteed of success for that goal. Your only responsibility was to be absolutely clear about exactly what it is that you would want to be, have, or do more than anything else in the world. What would it be?

Once you become perfectly clear about who you are and what you want personally, you can then move on to setting your business and financial goals.

Brenda Bence is an internationally-recognized branding expert, certified executive coach, professional speaker, and author of the award-winning *How YOU™ Are Like Shampoo* series of personal branding books.

With an MBA from Harvard Business School, Brenda's 25-year career has included developing mega brands for Fortune 100 companies across four continents and 50 countries. Combining her passion for brands with her passion for coaching, Brenda created the world's only personal branding system based on the same framework companies use to build successful mega brands.

Now, as President of Brand Development Associates International, Ltd. Brenda travels the world speaking, training, and coaching individuals and companies on how to achieve greater success through both corporate and personal branding. To find out more about Brenda's entertaining and engaging programs, visit or e-mail Brenda at the following:

Website: www.BrendaBence.com
E-mail: Brenda@BrendaBence.com
Phone: 312-242-1830

Chapter Nine

The Power and Purpose of Personal Branding

Brenda Bence

A Personal Branding Story Gone Wrong... and Then, *Very* Right

Alfred Nobel was a very successful and wealthy Swedish industrialist in the late 1800's. He was widely credited with inventing two things: dynamite and the detonator (the apparatus that causes dynamite to ignite from a distance.) He had made millions through these inventions, and he was living a wonderful millionaire's life.

Alfred's brother, Ludwig Nobel, who was also a well-known wealthy businessman, died in 1888. However, the obituary that showed up the next day in the newspaper was switched, and it was *Alfred's* obituary that appeared, not Ludwig's. So, Alfred Nobel had the rare opportunity of opening up the morning paper and reading his own life story.

Can you imagine how powerful that would be?

But, Alfred must have cringed when he read the headline of his obituary. It labeled him "The Merchant of Death" because of his work with dynamite and detonators. In that single moment, Alfred realized that everything he had done would forever associate his name – his personal brand – with death and destruction... unless he took control and did something about it.

So, he decided to change his personal brand. He made a plan to develop the Nobel Prizes for outstanding achievements in subjects he cared most about and, when he died in 1895, he left the bulk of his millions to the establishment of those prizes.

You've no doubt heard of the Nobel Prizes, but you may not have known about Nobel's connection with dynamite. That's because Alfred Nobel was successful in changing his personal brand and, today, his name continues to stand for what he wanted.

What Worked for Nobel Can Work for You, Too

You don't have to be a millionaire or a famous inventor to take charge of your personal brand. You, too, can take control of what you want to stand for and use your individual brand to improve every aspect of your life.

"But, Brenda," you might say, "you've got me all wrong! I'm not into self-promotion. I don't have – or even *want* – a personal brand."

Well, here's the truth: You already *have* a personal brand. That's because personal branding is "the way people perceive, think, and feel about you in relation to others." Since the people you interact with in all aspects of your life already have perceptions, thoughts, and feelings about you, the fact is you are automatically "branded" – just by virtue of being you.

The fundamental question is this: Do you have the personal brand you *want*? Is your individual brand bringing you greater success in life, or is it holding you back? Not knowing the answer to that question could mean the difference between a life you love living and a life that leaves you feeling lost.

Personal branding is all about your life purpose and the legacy you want to leave behind. The clearer you are about that purpose – what you're here for – the more fulfilling your life will be.

Take a Cue from Your Shampoo

So, how do you take control of this personal brand you already have? Do what big companies do!

Think about it: You're probably faithful to at least a couple of name brands. Maybe it's your favorite brand of double chocolate ice cream or a particular shampoo that you wouldn't dream of giving up. If you're like most people, you'll be loyal to those same brands over and over and over again.

So, if brands are so powerful that they grab our hearts and bring out that kind of loyalty - loyalty that keeps us reaching into our pocketbooks year after year – why can't we, as individuals, evoke that same kind of loyalty? If you were the "brand of choice" in your workplace, for example, what would that mean in terms of promotions, recognition, and higher pay? If you were the "brand of choice" in your community, what would that mean in terms of the relationships and opportunities that it would open up for you?

Now, of course, I'm not suggesting that you are a product like a carton of ice cream or a bottle of shampoo. But, the truth is that we are all *like* shampoo because, just as a shampoo must offer a benefit to improve your hair, you must also offer something of value to others. Taking charge of your personal brand is exactly how you become known for what you have to offer.

When you take the time to create the personal brand you *want*, "YOU™" – the trademarked you – can build meaningful connections at work and beyond. Then, just like you choose your favorite brand of shampoo from the shelf, the people you want to influence with your personal brand will choose YOU™.

Personal Branding is Powerful Stuff

As a vctcran corporate brander, I have spent more than 25 years defining, launching, and building brands all over the world using an established process and framework. And, I can tell you one thing for sure: Great brands don't become great brands by accident! It's only because of a tried-and-true process that the world's top brands become household names and make millions.

Several years ago, in my roles as a coach, trainer, and speaker, I began actively working with people to help them to reach their goals and develop their unique personal brands. I took that same tried and true corporate branding process and applied it to develop a *personal branding system* that thousands of people across the world have now used to better their careers and lives.

As a result, I've witnessed transformation after transformation in my clients. I've seen how creating a personal brand helps them expand their vision of what they can do and be in their lives. I have watched them build confidence as they become more aware of their talents and strengths. I have seen the satisfaction on their faces which comes from knowing they are on their way to reaching their full potential.

Five Tips for Mastering Your Personal Brand

So, how do you create a personal brand that will bring you more success and fulfillment in your life? There are many elements to my full personal branding system, but here are a few useful tips to get you started:

1) Remember: It's not all about you.
Some people believe that personal branding is self-centered and all about "me, me, me," but the truth is this: Good, strategic personal branding starts first and foremost with the "audience" for your personal brand - the people you most want to impact in your life. Just like a top, name-brand shampoo fills a consumer's need for shiny, healthy hair, you, too, must fill one or more of your audience's needs in order for your personal brand to be a success.

2) Find out how your audience perceives you *now*.
Since your personal brand exists in the minds of your audience, the only way to know if your brand is successful is to find out what your audience perceives, thinks, and feels about you right now. Listen and look for clues. If there is a gap between how your audience *currently* perceives you and how you *want* to be perceived, this is your chance to pinpoint what you want to change.

3) Define your personal brand – carefully.
While many people believe that personal branding is all about how you look or dress, true personal branding starts with developing a crystal clear definition of who you are and who you want to be. Until you define it, your brand is just a vague promise with no real foundation. Just as a good corporate marketer wouldn't dream of putting a product in the market without being clear on what that brand wants to stand for, you should do the same with your own brand.

4) Be consistent day-in and day-out.
To build a solid personal brand, it's critical to be consistent in how you communicate it. Think about it: If Nike's ads suddenly encouraged you to become a couch potato, you wouldn't know what to believe. Just like Nike consistently promotes its "Just Do It" attitude in all of its marketing activities, you, too, must be consistent every single day in how you present your personal brand to the world.

5) Be authentic.
Even though your personal brand is based on the needs of your audience, it never makes sense to pretend to be someone you're not. You won't be happy trying to remain consistent with a "fake" brand. So, the task is to find out what your audience needs, and align those needs with your own unique strengths and character traits. Your personal brand will then reflect who YOU™ really are.

Remember 24/7/365

Your personal brand is either working for or against you 24 hours a day, 7 days a week, 365 days a year. If you aren't taking control of it and consciously striving to define and communicate a brand that helps you reach your full potential, you may actually be damaging your brand and preventing yourself from living the life you desire. Use your brand like a compass to help you define your objectives in life and guide you in the direction you want to go. That's the power and purpose of personal branding.

Keith Ferrazzi, "the world's most connected individual" according to *Forbes* and *Inc.*, transformed professional networking with his bestselling book ***Never Eat Alone***. His new book, the #1 *New York Times* bestseller ***Who's Got Your Back?***, provides people with a do-it-yourself blueprint for creating "lifeline relationships" that offer the guidance, encouragement, and accountability needed to succeed. Keith has appeared on *Good Morning America, Larry King Live,* and *CNBC,* among other national media.

As founder and CEO of Ferrazzi Greenlight, Ferrazzi counsels the world's top enterprises on how to dramatically accelerate relationship development to drive sales, spark innovation, and create team cohesion. His Relationship Masters Academy helps business professionals build the deep network of relationships they need to exceed their goals. For more information and to download free resources, visit Keith at:

Website: *www.KeithFerrazzi.com*
E-mail: *kf@ferrazzigreenlight.com*
LinkedIn: *keithferrazzi*
Twitter: *@keithferrazzi*
Facebook: *keithferrazzi*
Phone: *310-913-2115*

Chapter Ten

Fulfill Your Purpose with Candor

Keith Ferrazzi

Excerpted from *Who's Got Your Back: The Breakthrough Program to Build Deep, Trusting Relationships that Create Success - And Won't Let You Fail*

As a young undergrad at Yale, I took an economics course from James Tobin, the late Keynesian scholar and Nobel Prize winner. I talked my way into his class even though I didn't remotely qualify for it, because I wanted to learn anything I could from a guy as brilliant as that. Not surprisingly, the class turned out to be way over my head; I logged a C minus, and even that was by the skin of my teeth. The good news is I got to talk about ideas with a Nobel Prize winner and even play poker with him. He usually won; I would go home with an empty wallet but a head flush with questions and ideas.

From Tobin I learned that in an ideal stock market, all the players would have complete and equal knowledge of the stocks they were trading—what Tobin called "perfect information." The opposite of perfect information—a handful of people making stock trades on information the rest of us don't have—is also known as insider trading. Not a good thing.

Nothing is ever perfect, of course, but the point is that for the whole system to work most effectively, everyone has to agree in principle on complete and honest disclosure. (Warren Buffett bases his investment decisions in part on whether he feels a company's executives are candid and not apt to sugarcoat problems.) Would you invest in the stock market of a developing country where you suspected the numbers reported by companies were outright lies? Of course not!

And so it is—or should be—in our personal and professional lives. Valuable feedback from others whom we respect, and who care about us and our careers (bosses, friends, colleagues, spouses, or even coaches and therapists), can help us become more aware of where we are, what we should be doing differently, what we should stop doing, and how we can perform better. The poet Robert Burns put it more succinctly: "To see ourselves as others see us! It would from many a blunder free us."

Openness, Honesty, and Candor

Opening yourself to feedback is also relatively risk-free. Because whatever our co-workers, associates, and friends are thinking about, they'll be thinking it anyway! Their candor won't change that. On the upside, it can open us up to opportunities we haven't seen before.

What do I mean by candor? Candor is the ability to engage in healthy, caring, purposeful criticism—as opposed to turf wars, nitpicking, or simply turning our backs and not communicating about issues at all. To me, candor is the greatest gift you can give if it comes from a place of caring about the other person enough to want her to get better. It's a two-way street, too—we need to be able to tell others the truth, and receive it in return.

Yet the single biggest issue I deal with in working with clients worldwide is the lack of open, honest, robust, respectful communication. Within the corporate world, the absence of candor is the single most corrosive cause of lackluster performance I know of—and the main culprit lurking behind that thing known as "office politics." A lack of candor breeds resentment and passive aggressive behavior.

So why don't we want to hear the truth? Because it can hurt!

We worry we'll hear something that contradicts our carefully constructed self-image. By the same token, we're deathly afraid of offending others by telling *them* the truth. As a result, we keep quiet, refrain from commenting, fudge our opinions, hedge our bets, soften our criticism or feedback, and reframe our real reactions with a more positive spin (sometimes we even lie). Being candid with one another could cost us our self-esteem, our job, even our friends. The whole thing is too risky!

Hey, these are all understandable fears.

My colleague at Greenlight Research, Dr. Mark Goulston, says, "Part of the reason we don't want to hear the truth is that we have a fear that it will metastasize through our entire being. So if I'm wrong about this one thing, I could be wrong about everything! In fact, every person is wrong about some things and right about others. Every person is very good at some things and not so good at others. Once we accept that **our shortcomings do not negate our merits**, we can compartmentalize criticism and not let it overwhelm us."

The Value of Full Disclosure

Being able to hear the truth about what others think of us, our actions, and our behaviors is essential. First, it's vital that we know the score, so that we have the opportunity to change our behavior if we're acting in an inappropriate or less-than-optimal way.

Second, in the end, the truth isn't going anyplace. Ignore it, and it will bite you in the bum. Repress it, and it will almost *always* seep out or erupt in one way or another—usually at the worst time possible—resulting in mediocre long-term performance. So many people labor under the assumption that if they just close their mouths, stay out of the line of fire, and put a muzzle on their true feelings, things will somehow fix themselves. Sorry, but problems get *worse* when they are kept under wraps.

Third, avoiding candor is deadly to our long-term success. Studies conducted since the 1970s make it clear that people who avoid conflict undermine both their relationships and their success. Candor involves engaging in real, tough, caring conversations. Employees who dodge genuine candor can become socially isolated from those around them. Avoiding transparency can undermine every aspect of your life, from the workplace to your home, whether it's a guy who goes to bed angry with his wife or a mother who looks the other way when her daughter repeatedly breaks curfew.

Whereas those who engage in transparency:

• Facilitate an overall understanding of everyone's perspectives. They listen attentively, don't just wait for their turn to talk, and are often the ones mediating a conversation with a clearer understanding of both parties' needs, wishes, and concerns. By not being fearful of expressing themselves, they can candidly express what they're hearing, and what their personal impressions and interpretations are of what's really being said.

• Are more capable of developing high-quality solutions. Because these folks tell it like it is (by not withholding information or playing politics), others tend to trust them to come up with unbiased, balanced solutions.

• Are more likely to build and maintain stronger relationships. People aren't worried what these folks think of them and their ideas—and as a result, people can more easily graduate to a trusting relationship with them without fearing what might be lurking underneath the surface.

- Are more competent and more respected. People **respect** the truth even when they may not want to hear it. Interestingly, those who tend to be more transparent <u>also</u> tend to spend less time beating around the bush, instead getting to the core of the issue at hand.

Even at Work?

Especially at work! I'm not saying you have to be candid with everyone right off the bat. Try it with people you trust and in places where there is little downside, such as asking your boss how you're doing on a specific project or task (you should do this constantly).

The key is to truly want to be a better employee—which starts from a personal desire to *always* be at the top of your game. Request feedback from the top, and make it easy for your boss to respond. Send him an e-mail in advance asking him to consider just one thing you could do to improve your job performance. Also, make sure the boss clearly describes the ultimate results he'll be measuring you on, and consistently report your progress toward those results in an e-mail (and verbally as well). Also, find out if your current trajectory is appropriate and if for any reason the workplace expectations have changed—because things *do* change, as everyone knows, and making assumptions is dangerous.

What if you slip up? Be the first one to come clean. Ultimately you'll be rewarded for your candor and courage if you proactively suggest how to fix the problem. Make sure to apologize for the mistake, and come up with a corrective action or solution to decrease the chances it will ever happen again. Now—live up to your promise!

Marion Richardson is a highly regarded, successful compliance and risk management professional in the health care industry. Marion's extensive management experience and her down-to-earth, practical approach to every day business situations make her a speaker to whom audiences can easily relate. Her warm style also makes her an outstanding mentor.

Marion has the distinct ability to connect with and motivate people, helping them to see their strengths and discover that the only limitations are those they impose upon themselves. Her gift for drawing out the best in others has helped her to create high-performing teams throughout her career.

Marion holds a paralegal degree, a certification as a Project Management Professional, and a Bachelor of Science degree in Technical Management. For more information, contact or visit Marion at the following:

Website: *www.MarionRichardson.com*
E-mail: *Marion@MarionRichardson.com*
Twitter: *@mentormarion*
Facebook: *MRichardson01*
Phone: *210-695-1553*

Chapter Eleven

A 7-Step Shortcut to Success

Marion Richardson

Time to Evaluate

Negativity can prevent us from exploring life to the fullest and bringing out the best in ourselves. We all go through phases when we feel overwhelmed or feel that we are lacking direction. Successful people aren't immune to those feelings. The difference is that they find the way to move past those phases quickly; they persevere, overcome obstacles, and stay focused on their objective.

I bet you can still remember the first person in your life who told you that you could not do something. Remember how that made you feel? We call these people "dream stealers." Erase those thoughts from your mind, as well as the people who influence you negatively. You have the ability to control your destiny and realize your dreams. The key to success is in understanding that you are not merely a spectator, but that you are the captain of your ship and only YOU can chart your course. Surround yourself with people who believe you can succeed.

All too often, we permit negative thoughts to permeate our minds. These negative thoughts can cause us to give up our aspirations, leaving us feeling defeated before we've even begun. Many of us look at successful people as being those who were in the right place at the right time. Are successful people just luckier than the rest of us? Absolutely not! Successful people are those who rise above their circumstances, learn from their failures, and seek out new opportunities, eager to make the most of them.

Breaking Out

I began my professional life with a high school diploma and a paralegal diploma. This was back in the days when a paralegal program consisted of nine months training, not the more intense form of the programs that you see today. In today's market, you may think you don't have a chance to succeed in the professional arena if you do not have a degree. Don't fall into the trap of believing that your professional career is doomed just because you don't have a formal education; that is far from the truth.

As life would have it, my education was interrupted due to a family medical situation and I kept delaying going back to school. I trudged to the same job - day in and day out, hoping that things would improve.

For most of my early working years, I reported to someone who dictated what I was to do and when I was to do it. Novelist Samuel Butler once made the acerbic observation that, "Life is one long process of getting tired." His statement seemed to sum things up for me at that point in my life.

I finally decided it was time to take charge of my life and learn a new skill. I woke up one day and decided, "TODAY is the day!" No more excuses; no more waiting. I thought to myself, "Why can't I do it? Why can't I become the person I have dreamed of being?" I knew there was a successful professional in me; I just hadn't taken the time to cultivate that person and find the right opportunities. And yes, I said "FIND!" Opportunity is out there, but it's up to us to make the most of it. We all have the ability...but sometimes we need a push to tap into it.

I was working for a very large insurance company and I asked my manager, a highly qualified computer programmer, to work with me for an hour each week to teach me computer programming. He agreed. As it turned out, something I had been reluctant to do - but did anyway - ended up resulting in endless possibilities and countless doors opening to new opportunities. I owe that manager a debt of gratitude. In addition to the one hour per week training session with him, I bought books and spent my "free" time learning everything I could about programming. I asked questions of every programmer I knew, eager to learn more.

Search Out an Advocate

The importance of having an advocate or mentor cannot be stressed enough. An advocate possesses the skills you want to acquire. Advocates promote your causes and are there to assist you in making your dreams come to fruition. They can be found anywhere - at work, church events, social gatherings, and networking events. I have found it's best to establish a personal rapport before enlisting someone as an advocate. Knowing an individual on a personal level provides better insight regarding the communication tools necessary for accurate messaging. Finding an advocate is not as difficult as you might think. Most people will feel honored that you think enough of their skills that you want to learn from them.

Determination = Success

I have found that there are seven components to success: show up, believe in yourself, focus, identify needed tools, join professional organizations and volunteer, create an action plan, and then put your plan into action.

1. Show Up
There is no substitute for this first component. Take responsibility for your future and be accountable. Don't wait until someone is ready to send an opportunity your way. Create your own opportunities. Go out and get what you want.

2. Believe in Yourself
You need to believe in yourself. Good self-esteem is contagious! If you present a "can do" attitude, others will follow your lead.

3. Have Focus
Focus on your goal. Focus will help you to put your attention where it needs to be and eliminate distractions. By focusing on your desired outcome, you'll avoid ever having to look back and wonder what happened to your dreams.

4. Identify Needed Tools
Is there a skill you need to acquire, an advocate you need to meet, a certification or affiliation that would prove beneficial to you? Do the necessary research; discover how to obtain the information, skills, or tools needed. There is a vast amount of information available to you through the internet and the connections you can make online. Take advantage of these free resources and put them to use.

5. Join Professional Organizations and Volunteer!
Volunteering provides many avenues of opportunity. In addition to learning skills and expanding your knowledge base, it also provides a great networking platform. Community events provide an ideal opportunity to connect with people from various backgrounds. You never know who you will meet or how those individuals might be able to assist you in your endeavors. Volunteering is not just good for you, but it's good for your community too.

Another outstanding way to make contacts is by joining professional organizations. Sharing ideas with like-minded individuals is stimulating and mutually beneficial. Get to know everyone and have a greater impact by joining the board of directors. Participation on a board immediately identifies you as an authority in your field.

6. Create an Action Plan
Identify where you want to be and determine how long it will take you to get there. It's important to attach a timeline to your plan, and particularly to each goal within your plan. Without a clear, well-defined plan and a deadline for reaching it, it is easy to become distracted.

7. Put Your Plan into Action
Move forward with your plan. Don't get bogged down with perfecting every detail. Being adaptable will make it easier for you to adjust to changes as they occur. Once you're on your way, you will gain increased confidence and motivation.

Where is Opportunity?

In short, opportunity is right in front of you. All you need to do is open the door. Opportunity has nothing to do with luck. Being in the right place at the right time is something that we control when we make ourselves available whenever opportunity knocks. Make your own luck. Seek out and exploit opportunities.

All of us have a purpose in life, and most of us discover our purpose while we are busy pursuing opportunities that come our way.

In Conclusion

You can make it happen. Identify your goals, obtain the required tools, and *move forward.* As President Teddy Roosevelt said, "In any moment of decision, the best thing you can do is the right thing, the next best thing is the wrong thing (but report it), and the worst thing you can do is nothing." Indecision can lead to paralysis. Don't be afraid to take a chance and try something new. Most people admit their greatest regrets are the things they never tried. Be the individual who greets an opportunity and runs with it.

Each of us is afforded opportunities every day to change our lives. Why not make the most of life and reach for the golden ring? There is nothing stopping us except for ourselves. If someone told me years ago that I would become a published author, I probably would have told them they were crazy! Yet, here I am... achieving that goal. You can do *anything* you set your mind to, and although it may not always be effortless, the rewards outweigh the fears by far.

Christopher Gomez's motto? "When life hands you lemons, go fund a beverage company!" Chris is a highly-focused business expert with extensive experience working with start-ups. His expertise is in helping small businesses stream-line their services and products, better define their niches, and expand their market and reach effectively, especially into Asia.

He is also a well-connected angel investor, seeking high-value ideas from entrepreneurs, and is actively involved in funding media projects. He is the co-founder of "Launch", a power-networking group, and is also the founder of "Filmcamp" - an educational conference that reveals the mysteries of film making and the film business.

Chris brings humor and real world anecdotes to his presentations and mentoring sessions. Please visit or contact Chris at:

Website: *enginealpha.com*
E-mail: *connect@enginealpha.com*
Twitter: *@chrisgomez*
Skype: *enginealpha*

Chapter Twelve

Are You Ready to Give Up the "Rat Race"?

Christopher Gomez

Tired of the rat race, slaving in your office day in and day out, struggling to pay the bills at the end of every month? Now, imagine living like this for the rest of your life! It doesn't have to be this way. If you've ever wondered what it's like to be your own boss, there's no time like the present to give it a shot – IF you are prepared and ready to get the help you need to assure your success!

In good times and in bad, entrepreneurs and upstarts have found tremendous success. Google, Microsoft, Apple, and FedEx were all started during economic downturns...and they all seem to be doing *incredibly well!* In *Entrepreneur Magazine*, marketing consultant Greg Digneo cited three reasons to start a business, even in challenging economic times. First, you'll develop great habits. Being forced to focus on your bottom line will help you to increase profits. Next, you'll have to create great products and services. Competitive times make for great product development and service-oriented success. And third, if you can make it during tough times, you'll positively THRIVE when the economy picks up.

More than two-thirds of the world's millionaires are simple entrepreneurs and salespeople, living in average homes and operating small businesses. Putting together a startup business can help you to solve your financial challenges. As a small business consultant, the most consistent question I hear is, "How do I get started?"

Some people panic just *thinking about* starting their own business. They focus on all the reasons why a business might fail. They sometimes think they don't have the time or expertise to start something big. If this describes you, don't feel intimidated; your business doesn't have to be BIG to be successful. Here are six benefits to starting your own small business.

1. A Small Business Can Be Run From Home

A small business is one that employs fewer than ten people. Most small businesses, however, consist of just one person – the business owner. These individuals start small and grow. Many small businesses start out as part-time jobs, such as selling Avon products or dabbling in real estate. Others come to life in their owner's garage, – which is how Steve Wozniak and Steve Jobs created Apple Computers.

J.K. Rowling, author of the popular *Harry Potter* books, also started very small. She wrote *Harry Potter* from her desk at home and at the coffee shop down the street. She finally sold her book and the rest, as they say, is history! Think about it; if millions of entrepreneurs have succeeded in starting a small business, then you can, too!

2. You Can Succeed Regardless of Your Education

When people tell me they are intimidated by their lack of education, I tell them about Sir Richard Branson, owner of the massive Virgin Group of companies. He never finished college; in fact, he was dyslexic and performed poorly in school. But, he used his ability to connect with people to launch his first successful magazine when he was just sixteen. By 2009, his net worth stood at more than *$2.4 billion!* Pretty good for someone who didn't do well in school, don't you agree?

Never let your educational background hold you back from starting something big. Education is still important, but as an entrepreneur, you can take advantage of adult education classes, books, mentors, and online education courses that can offer the specific training that you might need.

3. Staying Small Means You Can Offer More

A small business is easier and more enjoyable to run than you might think. Regardless of the business, if you stay small you'll have more opportunities to build great relationships with your clients.

The owners of bigger companies often meet customers and clients on the first day, only to pawn their new clients off to their assistants or project managers. It's a cold setup that can dampen customer satisfaction.

When your small business stays small, however, you can meet people face-to-face and spend quality time with them. Remember, prospective clients value trust much more than technical expertise. Keeping a small business small lets you offer personal services and build stronger relationships with your clients. And, if your company grows and you hire employees, your office can become one big, happy family, a luxury that many of the world's larger companies can't afford.

4. Small Businesses Offer Greater Flexibility and Are More Adaptable

Some people tell me they are hesitant to open a small business because they think it's risky to do so during tough economic times. This is not true. The need for startups that offer products and services at a good value is greater than ever. Besides, economic crunches hit the biggest companies the hardest. Everyone saw the big banks and car companies in the U.S. crumble when the recession hit early in 2009, while smaller businesses fared better. In fact, small U.S. towns that ran entirely on small businesses even thrived during that time! Those that relied on one big factory were hit the hardest.

Small businesses can adapt more easily to changing economic trends. They can spot opportunities and react faster than big companies. For instance, independent players in the real estate market are doing much better than real estate companies in the U.S. today, simply because they're not bogged down by operational laws and office regulations. To them, times are only hard if they choose to let them be. For small businesses, the economy can be what you make of it.

5. Small Businesses Can Focus on Specialization

Staying small lets you serve a specific slice of the market, or niche, where you can make a name for yourself. For instance, if you wanted to put up a small eatery, you wouldn't want to offer burgers, pizza, tacos, pasta, salads, and Chinese food at the same time. This is also called "spreading yourself too thin." When you specialize in a specific niche - such as serving flavored pancakes – it's easier for you to consistently improve your business. As your popularity grows, more customers will start to look for your particular pancakes in different parts of town. This is when you open another branch -- and another, and another!

Shops that only offer one item, whether it is souvenirs, shoes, burgers, or coffee, have found that specializing helps them to be more successful. Starbucks is a great example of a business that kept it simple. Imagine what Starbucks would be like if it offered, in addition to its coffee menu, a library, a souvenir shop, and a few poker tables! The popular coffee franchise would probably be much less successful, since the broad, unwieldy setup would be hard to replicate all over the world. Instead, their menu centered on coffee and offered fast, friendly service. Their setup was so easily replicated that within a few years there was a Starbucks in almost every corner of the world. Specialization is what made Starbucks the most popular coffee shop all over the world.

6. Specialization Can Help Your Small Business Go Global

The more you specialize, the more your client base will grow...helping you to reach beyond your city and country. Specialization can help your small business go global. Thanks to the Internet, you can find people and companies all over the world who are interested in doing business with YOU!

Apple Computers didn't really take off until Steve Jobs streamlined it. It started off as a mere computer company in the 80's and took the market by storm. But, after the company made the mistake of firing Steve Jobs - one of its founders - they began to expand their product lines recklessly, which caused the company to tank in the market.

When Steve Jobs came back on board, he immediately began streamlining Apple, successfully restoring it to the company it used to be. They began to specialize in only a few select product lines instead of generalizing, trying to be all things to all people. Today, people all over the world have iPods, and Apple reaches all its customers with such ease that it doesn't even need to attend expos anymore.

When you stick to your special niche, you have the opportunity to develop your own standards, play by your own rules, and even tweak your business to be consistent with international standards.This alone is one of the greatest opportunities you'll discover as a small business owner - the opportunity to catapult your small business onto the world stage!

Build Your Own Dream Team

When you decide to start a business, get help. You can't be expected to know everything you need to know to start and run a business. Getting qualified help at the start will save you untold money and time. Build your very own Dream Team! When starting a business, you'll have many aspects to consider, such as legal, marketing, and financial matters. No one expects you to be an expert in all these fields. Find someone who has done what you want to do and hire them as your mentor. Understand the importance of building the right team to help you get your new business off the ground and keep it growing for years to come.

It all starts with you. In the United States alone, someone starts a small business every eleven seconds. The first step is right in front of you now; why wait?

What do you get when you mix a professional beach volleyball player with a chemist? You get **Barbara Khozam**, a speaker who understands energy, determination, and the importance of pursuing your purpose. Though she excelled as a chemist, with a B.S. in Chemistry, Barbara found her true purpose when she began training, speaking, and motivating audiences.

Barbara is an internationally recognized speaker and trainer who has presented to hundreds of audiences worldwide. Her presentations offer a unique blend of humor and experience cultivated from time spent in the worlds of both business and professional sports. Barbara tackles serious topics with down-to-earth presentations rich with humor and candor.

She brings an indomitable winner's attitude to all of her presentations. For information, call or visit Barbara at:

Website: www.barbarakhozam.com
Email: Barbara@BarbaraKhozam.com
Phone: 619-572-1117

Chapter Thirteen

Forget Baditude; Get SHAZAMitude!!!!

Barbara Khozam

"The only difference between a good day and a bad day is your attitude." Dennis S. Brown

Remember your senior year; the awkwardness, the lack of confidence, trying so hard to fit in? Before my senior year, I was painfully shy. What was I afraid of? Maybe it was just my nature, but I kept to myself, feeling so different from the other kids in school.

The Day of Transformation

Then, something happened that changed everything. I saw a sticker on a classmate's notebook that read, "Why be Normal?" Was that my problem? Had I been stuck inside myself because I was trying to fit in and be "normal?!" That sticker must have given me the permission I needed to become myself... the "real" me... as I instantly realized I didn't HAVE to be "normal." My mother instantly noticed the change in me; she said it was as if a different girl came home from school that day!

To embrace my new "philosophy", I got personalized license plates: "LMRN B Y" (Why Be Normal... backwards). It looked awesome on my 1972 peach Ford Pinto! This fed my new sense of self, my inner strength. It was something more powerful than just a positive attitude.

Years later, my father accidentally referred to my husband as "Shazam" instead of Khozam. Friends started calling me "Mrs. Shazam." The nickname stuck and a new concept was born; my powerful, positive attitude became SHAZAMitude!"

"SHAZAMitude" goes beyond a positive attitude; it's springing up from your pillow, looking forward to each new day, eager to discover what's in store, and embracing the opportunities that await you. That's "SHAZAMitude"; looking for the gusto in the every day existence and saying, "I'll have that!"

How You Can Develop SHAZAMitude

SHAZAMitude is an attitude of power. It means we respect ourselves. It's standing up for our rights without stepping on the rights of others. It's suspending critical judgment. It's NOT ego-driven arrogance, deluded self-importance, apologetic communication, or letting others walk all over you.

One of my seminar attendees said that to him, "SHAZAMitude means I am in control of a dynamic, positive, powerful, meaningful, and intelligent approach to everything I do." Embracing SHAZAMitude will give you confidence, awareness, and a greater sense of overall happiness. At the core of SHAZAMitude is **"SHAZAM,"** a perspective and attitude that anyone can develop.

S: Strength

The "S" in SHAZAM stands for **strength of character**. Are you in touch with your core values and do you live your life according to those values? A lot of people say their #1 value and priority in their lives is their family, yet they spend twelve or more hours a day at work. They are not being true to their core values, which can lead to feelings of low self-esteem.

We each have a set of values, and we use these values to help us make decisions. We weigh factors such as family, honesty, respect, compassion, humor, etc., and the decisions we make based on these qualities determine how we live our lives. Without knowing your own values, you may feel lost and vulnerable, and live your life according to other people's values or expectations.

Z-TIP: *Adopt a SHAZAMitude Attitude: If you do NOT know what your values are, you can discover them by doing the following exercise:*

- Make a list of all the positive traits you value in others – traits you would like to have.

- Print or handwrite them on a card. Have the card duplicated and laminated.

- Post the cards where you will be sure to see them throughout your day – on your desk, in your wallet, on the bathroom mirror, even on the refrigerator door. You will consistently be reminded of all the positive qualities and values that you want to develop.

Focusing your attention on these values will help you to manifest them in your own life. My clients are always amazed at how quickly this technique works to help them become the person they want to be. You'll be amazed, too!

H: Humor

A sense of humor can keep us from getting worked up over small things or taking them personally. When we lighten up, we become less stressed and more confident. People who laugh often are happier and more successful in ALL AREAS of their lives. Successful people make more money. Get in touch with your inner child and remember to laugh! Try to keep your sense of humor at all times.

Z-TIP*: My mom always said "Kill 'em with kindness." I do and it works. Every time someone says something negative, answer with something positive. If they say "I hate my job," say, "I LOVE my job." If they say, "I hate this weather; it's so hot outside," answer with, "Really? I love this heat! It feels good to sweat!" If you are nice to someone who is consistently negative, they will stop coming to you because – to them - you are no fun! They will prefer to find someone who will share in their misery.*

A: Assertiveness

Our goal is to be assertive, rather than aggressive or passive. However, assertiveness does not work the same on everyone. One of the keys to successful communication is to communicate with others in their own style. It is up to us to adapt. If a person with whom we are communicating is more aggressive, we may need to speak faster and be more direct. If the person is more passive, we may need to slow ourselves down a bit. And, if the approach you are using is not working, try something else!

Z-TIP*: When you need to assert yourself, especially when you need to say "NO!" use this simple "YES" formula"*

1. *Say "**Yes**"; agree and acknowledge their request.*

2. ***E****xplain your situation.*

3. ***S****olve the problem by proposing an alternative solution.*

If someone says "I need you to make 500 copies right now," you might say, "I understand you need 500 copies. I'm working on a project for my boss that's due in 30 minutes. I can help you in 30 minutes, or perhaps you can find someone else to help you immediately." The key to success is being assertive with regard to a solution. That will also take you out of a passive/aggressive dialogue.

NOTE: The first time you use this on someone they may be surprised by your new assertiveness. Just go back to steps #1 and #3 by saying "You're right, I have always done it for you. Today is different; I could have it for you after

4:00." Difficult people will test you at least three times, maybe even more. You'll need to be consistent until they accept your new SHAZAMitude!

Z: Zeal

Have you ever noticed which behavior is more contagious – positive or negative? The truth is that negativity is extremely contagious. If you wake up to the morning news, your day will start with negative thoughts of death, illness, and despair. At work, your colleagues might say "I hate my boss, I hate my job, I hate YOU!" Before long, you start thinking, "I hate MY boss, MY job....and I HATE MYSELF!" Negativity is extremely contagious. But, positive behavior, a can-do attitude, energy, and passion can be contagious too. Understand that when the world around you dwells on negativity, it can be harder to focus on the positive.

Z-TIP: The next time you wake up and you have a "baditude," low energy, and negative thoughts, FAKE IT! Many successful people know the benefits of "Fake it till you Make it!" Act as if you have all the energy in the world; wear brighter colors and a smile. One of my clients admitted she'll wear bright underpants just to perk herself up! And, it's not possible to feel sleepy or stressed when you have a big, contagious smile on your face! Plus, you'll be helping others. Exercise will help, too. Making our bodies move produces endorphins, which cause positive thoughts and stress reduction.

A: Acceptance

Accept the fact that not everyone will appreciate your new SHAZAMitude. When you first assert yourself and set your boundaries, people may think you have lost your mind! Know this, and know that you are indeed on a path to a better life. Stick to it!

*Z-TIP: The next time you find yourself with expectations – others **should** be a certain way or **should** have done this or that - STOP and PAUSE. Realize that people are different. Others will begin to accept you more as you show greater acceptance of them.*

M: Magic

When you have strength in your values, maintain a sense of humor, are assertive and positive in your communication, and are accepting of yourself and others, the results will be magical. Your new SHAZAMitude will carry you toward greater success and satisfaction in your work and at home.

Z-TIP: Understand that changing your behavior takes time. It takes about thirty consecutive days to create a new habit. That is also what you can expect when waiting for others to get used to YOUR new behavior (even longer if you are not consistent). This transformation is a process. Be consistent and persistent in your actions and – before you know it – you'll wake up every day with a powerful SHAZAMitude!

Fred Wikkeling has traveled internationally as a successful inspirational and motivational speaker and writer. His insightful book, ***Look Up See the Difference,*** has been met with rave reviews worldwide. Fred is a Certified Instructor for the Napoleon Hill, (***Think and Grow Rich***), Foundation and for Personality Insights, the premier company that administers the D.I.S.C. Personality Profile assessment. His Positive Mental Attitude message is aired on radio talk show **www.WLTH1370.com**.

Why is Fred in demand? The bottom line is that Fred delivers the quality answers and excellence that helps people improve all aspects of their lives. His popular presentations are fun and insightful and are always met with recognition and approval. His audiences feel secure, appreciated and assured. For more information, visit:

Website: www.discpeople.com
E-Mail: fredwikkeling@discpeople.com
LinkedIn: fredwikkeling
Twitter: @FredWikkeling
Facebook: fredwikkeling
Phone: 408-813-6609

Chapter Fourteen

D.I.S.C.over Yourself & Others

Fred Wikkeling

"If I understand you and you understand me, doesn't it make sense that we can work more effectively together?" Dr. Robert A. Rohm

I'd like to invite you to a workshop. It's right here – on these pages! I'm about to share information with you that will benefit you for *the rest of your life.*

All human beings have a dominant communication trait. The four basic traits are: the "Driver," the "Inspirational," the "Supportive" and the "Cautious" personalities. The four "DISC" styles apply to all races, genders, and nationalities. Based on these one-word descriptions, would you say are you a "D," "I," "S," or a "C"?

I wished I had discovered it when I was four years old instead of fifty-three! I passionately believe that everyone on earth would benefit from learning the DISC system. In fact, every mother should have her child assessed at the age of four. Get to know the people in your life better. Come and join my Workshop.

Welcome to the DISC Workshop

Sit down, relax, and take several deep breaths. You will discover how to quickly identify people's communication styles. After you grasp the concept, you'll be able to think back and identify the personality traits of your mother and father, your brothers and sisters, and all the people you know. You will be able apply this skill set with every person you meet *from now on!*

Let's Start with Two Questions

Are you *introverted* or *extroverted?* Introverts are more reserved, they move at a slower pace... they even talk slower and softer. Extroverts are outgoing and fast-paced...and talk faster and louder. Sometimes people think they are both, as they function differently in different situations. If that's you, just pick one group. You can always change you mind later.

Are you *people-oriented* or *task-oriented?* People-oriented people want to have fun. If invited to a social function, they are eager to attend, even if it means stopping whatever they were doing. Task-oriented people, however, complete projects. They would never consider dropping what they were doing to attend a function! Again, pick the one you are most likely to be.

Imagine we are in a room that is divided into four groups. The first group is the **outgoing, task-oriented** people. They will sit in the top, left section of the room. They are the "D's," because they are *Drivers*. They are always ready to go, so we will give them the color green. Their defining symbol is the exclamation point! D's are demanding; they say it's all about "The Bottom Line," "Just do it," "Do it now," or "Do it MY way." They live to win. They love to ask, "WHAT?" as in "What's up?"

Picture those who are **outgoing** and **people-oriented** in the top, right-hand section of the room. These are the "I's," because they are *Inspirational.* We'll make them red, because they love to be noticed. They are easily spotted because they love stars – wearing stars, star tattoos, star earrings, and lots of "bling." They are smooth talkers... influential and persuasive. I's live to have fun. They love to ask, "Who?" as in "Who is that?"

Visualize putting the third group in the bottom, right-hand section of the room. These are the people who are **reserved** and **people-oriented**. These are the "S's." They are *Supportive.* S's are calm, so we'll make them blue, like a calm sea. The plus and minus signs + are assigned to S's. This is because they are easily persuaded and change their minds often. S's are the sweetest people; they live to please and serve. S's favor the question "How?" as in "How can I help you?"

Finally, imagine the fourth group in the bottom, left-hand section of the room. These people are **reserved** and **task-oriented**. They are the "C's." C's are Cautious; we'll make them yellow, just like a caution light! The C's use phrases like, "It is better to be safe then to be sorry."

They are always right. The question mark "?" identifies C's as they always ask "why?"

Note the beginning letter of each personality type starts with the letter of each personal trait.

D's	I's	S's	C's
Dominant	Inspiring	Supportive	Cautious
Demanding	Influencing	Stable	Competent
Doer	Impressionable	Shy	Careful
*Defiant	*Illogical	*Sucker	*Cold

Negative Trait

Is it becoming clearer to you which group you favor? For a simple-to-understand chart, visit my website at **www.DISCPeople.com.** You'll also find a FREE mini-personality analysis there as well as a 4-part relationship exercise.

Basic Motivation

Each group is motivated in different ways. Understanding what motivates an individual will help you when working with them. *Give them **Motivation** for positive results:*

D's: Challenges, Choices and Control.
I's: Recognition, Approval, and Popularity
S's: Security, Appreciation and Assurance
C's: Quality answers, Excellence and Value

D's and I's believe rules are made to be broken, so they make up their own rules. C's and S's follow rules closely.

The D's and I's get in trouble at school for misbehaving and talking in class. The C and S groups seldom get in trouble. S's are "touchy-feely" people who live for peace and love hugs.

C's are cautious and prepared for emergencies; in fact, a lot of C's have flashlights placed several places in their homes.

"Opposites attract and then attack." Most people marry or are with someone who has diagonally opposite traits. D's and S's are usually attracted to each other and C's and I's are usually attracted to each other. Look at your situation; is your significant other diagonally opposite of your personality?

...That Reminds Me of Two Stories

#1. The Frog & The Scorpion: There once was a scorpion that was both *outgoing* and *people-oriented.* He moved quickly and was eager to get across the pond. "Hey, Mr. Frog," he said. "I need to get to the other side of the pond. Can you give me a ride on your back?" Mr. Frog thought this was a great opportunity to *Serve* and *Please,* so he agreed.

Being Cautious, the frog remembered that scorpions sting frogs. As S's are inclined to do, Mr. Frog changed his mind. He said to Mr. Scorpion, "If I give you a ride on my back, you will sting me and I'll drown."

Illogical Mr. Scorpion replied, "If I were to sting you, we would both drown. My goal is to get to the other side, too!" Being ***Supportive***, Mr. Frog agreed. As they approached the center of the pond, Mr. Scorpion stung Mr. Frog. Mr. Frog asked, "Why did you sting me? Now we'll both drown!" "You knew I was a scorpion when you met me and you knew that's what scorpions do," he replied.

The moral is that *we act according to our dominate trait*. Recognizing and understanding our traits help us to become better communicators.

#2. The DISC System Solves a Family's Communication Challenge: At a trade show, I met colleague whom I observed be a C type. As we spoke, she asked "Why" a lot. She gave me the impression that she was Careful and Cautious. She said she had a difficult time home-schooling her son. Her son is not cooperative and gives her a difficult time. She did not know what to do. I asked if her son was outgoing and task-oriented. She said yes, definitely.

It was clear she is C and her son is a D. I recognized and related well to her son's ***Defiant*** behavior. I stayed in trouble in at school I have both the D & I traits. Thinking back, most of my teachers had the C traits, though I was unaware at the time.

I suggested to my colleague that she change her approach with her son. Instead of telling him what to do, she should ask him what to do and give him choices. Doing this would make him feel he was in **Control** and would **Challenge** him to do better and get straight A's. This is all I suggested. The next day, I saw my colleague. She was exhilarated because her son's behavior had improved *overnight!* She said, "DISC really works. When you change, the world will change with you.

Put DISC to Use in YOUR Life!

In this "workshop," you have seen, heard, experienced, and have come to understand the basics of DISC in a very short time. Of course, experiencing a "live workshop" will be so much more fun, valuable and beneficial. You will get support and enjoy interaction with other DISC groups.

Get started with the online questionnaires today! You'll be impressed when you receive your own personalized detailed DISC report. The DISC system is more than 90% accurate! When the student is ready, the teacher appears. I've enjoyed sharing this workshop with you and look forward to the day we meet.

Fred Wikkeling is a Certified Instructor for the Napoleon Hill Foundation. Napoleon Hill is the author of the classic best seller, **Think and Grow Rich.** Fred teaches "The Seventeen Principles for Success." Napoleon Hill said, *"What the mind of man or woman can conceive and believe, they will achieve."*

Barbara Wilson has enjoyed a distinguished career as a teacher, human resource professional, and trainer. She uses her expert communication skills to engage audiences while educating and entertaining them. Her keynotes and seminars focus on relationship building, communication, and time management.

As a success coach, Barbara helps people find their unique talents and apply them effectively to the career best suited for them.

Barbara has earned a master's degree in international administration and a bachelor's degree in German and business. She has been certified as a Senior Professional in Human Resources. Visit Barbara at:

Website: www.BarbaraAnnWilson.com
E-mail: Barb@BarbaraAnnWilson.com,
LinkedIn: barbaraannwilson
Twitter: @coachbwilson
Phone: 248-763-6151

Chapter Fifteen

Following Your Dream

Barbara Wilson

"I just can't take it anymore," Sandy, a freckled-faced thirty-eight year-old nurse administrator sobbed as she anxiously wrung her hands. "They keep telling me I'm a bad manager and they sent me to this class to 'fix' me."

Here I was, in Bloomington, Illinois, teaching a class on how to manage difficult employees. I asked Sandy about her likes and dislikes, her dreams and goals. As she told me about her current job, she described a very real nightmare.

"Sandy, why did you decide on nursing as a career?" Her brow arched. Her eyes lit with delight as she talked about her passion for patient care. When I asked her if she liked managing people she cringed and once again fought back tears. "I took the administrative position because it paid more. But I hate it."

Sandy had lost her dream. Could I help her find it again?

"Sandy, what would happen if you asked your employer for a demotion?" Several seconds of silence followed. She looked puzzled. *People don't do that, do they?*

"You love *caring* for people, not *managing* them. If your employer won't give you a demotion, could you find a job someplace else in patient care?" As we worked through her options, Sandy perked up. Determination coursed through her. A plan formed. By the end of the seminar she knew what she needed to do and was ready to do it. She thanked me profusely and gave me a glowing review.

It had been an "Aha" moment for Sandy, but also for me. You see, in helping her live her dream, I was living my own. I'd taken a week's vacation from my high-paying, high-stress job to pursue my dream of becoming a public speaker and success coach. This was my first class; Sandy was my first official protégé. Suddenly, all my previous work experience came together and made sense. I breathed a contented sigh and thought: *I'm exactly where I am supposed to be.*

Do you spring up out of bed each morning feeling that you are doing what you are supposed to be doing? Are you living your dream, fulfilling the purpose for which you feel you were created?

I believe each of us has a unique purpose, a dream to live. The Bible says that God prepared "good works" in advance for us to do. But what are those "good works?" What is your purpose and how do you find it? You can start by following your "D.R.E.A.M."

D: Discern your Passions, Gifts, and Skills

We each have passions, gifts, and skills. Is there something you enjoy doing so much that you would do it for free? Do you lose track of time doing it? What do you read or talk about most? These are our passions.

Our gifts are talents or aptitudes we are naturally good at – as if we are hard-wired for them. My oldest son plays music by ear. He rarely pays attention to the notes on the page. He intuitively replicates the sounds and rhythms he hears with ease. That's a gift.

We acquire skills or knowledge through training and education. Some neurolinguists believe that with enough repetition, we can train our brains to do anything. While that may be true, it requires less effort to acquire a skill if it is in an area in which we naturally excel. For example, my sister is a gifted athlete; she excels in every sport she tries. I can acquire a certain amount of skill in sports, but since I missed out on the athletic gene, it takes me twice as much effort just to make the team.

A myriad of assessment tools are available to help you to identify your passions, gifts and skills. Find a competent career counselor or coach to help guide you through this process. These trained professionals can give you valuable insight about the kind of job in which you would excel.

R: Release Your Fears

According to Brian Tracy, fear is the single biggest obstacle to success. Of course you have fears as you consider your dream; we all do. The trick is to play that fear out and look for possibilities. My fears included: What if my husband loses his job? (He'll get another.) What if we can't make it without my steady paycheck? (We'll cut our expenses until we do.) What if I get sick? (I'll recover.) What if I fail? (There is no such thing as failure... only the inability to learn from experience.)

The "First Lady of American Journalism" Dorothy Thompson once said "Only when we are no longer afraid do we begin to live." Release your fears and live out your purpose.

E: Encourage Yourself

The best way to encourage yourself is through a positive mental attitude. Success pioneer Napoleon Hill said, "A positive mental attitude is the single most important principle in the science of success."

How do you keep a positive attitude? Here are three ways:

- First, surround yourself with people who believe in you and support you. We need people around us who will cheer us on and remind us that "We can do it!"

- Second, interview people who do what you think you'd like to do. Ask them what they like and dislike about their situation and what steps they took that allowed them this opportunity. This technique helped me to discern that I did not want to be a school teacher, but that I did want to be a public speaker.

- Third, take small steps each day towards your goals and celebrate small victories. For many people the staircase is so overwhelming that they don't even take the first step. Keep your focus on one step at a time and celebrate each completed step.

A: Adjust as Needed

The day after I tendered my resignation and set off to build my consulting business, another dream came to fruition - the stick turned blue. My husband and I were thrilled that I was pregnant. This was part of the plan. But a few weeks later, when I went to the doctor, our plans took an unexpected turn.

"Twins? Can you check again, doctor?"

"Look for yourself," he grinned, and turned the ultrasound monitor towards me. Sure enough, at just seven weeks pregnant, I saw two tiny hearts beating on the screen.

To kick start my speaking business, I'd signed a contract with a national training company that required me to travel nationwide. And, I had to provide my availability six months in advance. Those little heart beats labeled me as a "high-risk" pregnancy, which meant no more travel. Also, three months prior to my due date, I'd need to stop working altogether.

Did these new challenges mean that I had to give up public speaking and coaching? Not at all. We just made adjustments. I was able to have it all, just not all at once. Now, four years later, my twins are headed to preschool and I've got plenty of speaking engagements and coaching clients.

M: Mind your Motives

"You are not here merely to make a living. You are here to enable the world to live more amply, with greater vision, and with finer spirit of hope and achievement. You are here to enrich the world. You impoverish yourself if you forget this errand." - Woodrow Wilson

In my twenty-five plus years experience in the workforce, I've seen many dreams die due to misplaced motives. Let me give a gentle warning here. Is the goal of your dream to achieve money, fame, or power? Author and speaker John Ortberg states, "For many, careers become the altar on which people sacrifice their lives." While material wealth and notoriety may be a by-product of following your passions, if these are your sole motivations, you'll sacrifice your life on that "career altar."

Ask yourself, "Why do I want this dream? What do I ultimately hope to accomplish?" For me, my motivation is deeply rooted in my faith. I seek to honor God in all I do. This is reflected in my personal mission statement: To positively impact lives through inspiring people to peak performance.

Finally, be persistent. You probably won't find your dream overnight. Set realistic goals. Expect setbacks and delays to be part of the process. Moses was 80 before God called him to lead his people out of Egypt. Julia Child was over 50 when she published her first cookbook. Ray Kroc was 52 when started the McDonald's franchise. Every person who has achieved their dream has a story to tell about the obstacles they overcame. Persistence is what separates the dreamer from those living their dreams. As you persist, may your dreams become your reality.

Hugh Zaretsky is a "Recovering Corporate Executive," who has consulted for Fortune 500 companies and helped lead his teams to win CIO magazine's Top 100 award. He is an expert in corporate acquisitions and shutdowns.

He shows entrepreneurs how to "Fire Their Boss" and achieve financial freedom through real estate investing and business ownership. Hugh made it his mission to help people who relied on their jobs to take care of them... those who would have no recourse should their job ever let them down.

Hugh is a sought after coach, consultant, and professional speaker. Hugh's impressive client list includes major corporations and Wall Street analysts, as well as some of the top entrepreneurial companies including Get Motivated and the Learning Annex. Visit Hugh at:

Websites:	*www.hughzaretsky.com*
	www.StepsToFireYourBoss.com
Email:	*hugh@hughzaretsky.com*
	KickMe@hughzaretsky.com
	(for motivation)
Twitter:	*@HughZaretsky*
Phone:	*646-584-5818*

Chapter Sixteen

Fire Your Boss & Turn Your Passion into Profits

Hugh Zaretsky

Sept 11th, 2001 is a date that everyone will always remember. It forever changed the way we think about our world, our safety, and our security. This was the first time I had seen a company put employees in harms way. In the midst of the chaos that will always be known as "9-11," I decided that if I was going to succeed, it would be up to me. The business world was in for some major changes, and I decided I no longer wanted to be a part of Corporate America. I made the decision to fire my boss.

Firing your boss is one of the greatest feelings in the world. This is the day most people dream about. I can tell you, it is the best decision that I have ever made. I made this decision as I snuck past the National Guard barricade on 9/11 to get back to my JOB. My company's headquarters on the West Coast had asked me to send one of my employees back to the office which was, essentially, in the middle of a war zone. I refused to put one of my team members in harm's way, so I went instead. As I snuck past the roadblock staffed with soldiers carrying automatic weapons, I decided that I needed to put my plan into action; I would leave the corporate world. I've never looked back.

Being confident is admirable, but taking such a major step with your career requires more than resolve and a serene smile. Watching your aspirations and perhaps your life savings going down the drain as you struggle to become a successful entrepreneur will quickly wipe any smile off your face. Firing your boss is an exciting proposition; you just want to be sure you have a solid plan before you make such a bold move!

Today, I help others to "Fire Their Boss." It's the first step toward turning your passion into a profitable business. There are landmines waiting for new business owners and entrepreneurs. There are many things that can sabotage your desire to take control of your life. The landmines you want to avoid are things like not spending enough time laying out your business plan, failing to set specific goals, and not doing market research to determine the profitability of your business venture. It's possible to turn your passion into profit, but it helps to stack the deck in your favor. You can do that by working with someone who has done it before. They know about the landmines and can help you to avoid costly mistakes along your new, exciting path. I have been there before and succeeded, time and time again. I can show you what to do, how to do it, and what to avoid. Are you ready to *FIRE YOUR BOSS?*

There are many steps to take when preparing to strike out on your own. For a full list of these, visit: **www.StepsToFireYourBoss.com.** For now, let's concentrate on those things that most people tend to forget at a time like this.

Do Your Research to Find Your Magic Number

Your magic number represents the amount of money your venture will need to earn in order for you to fire the boss and start working for yourself full time. Your magic number should take into account the amount required to cover your current bills and replace your income. One of the items that people forget to include in this number is health insurance. As an employee, your company probably covers all or a percentage of your current insurance costs. You will need to add that cost to your number, along with self-employment tax, social security, and your own retirement plan costs.

Re-evaluate your current monthly spending habits and your budget. Determine where you can start reducing some of your monthly expenses. The more money you can reduce from your monthly budget, the faster you can fire your boss. The dividends of working for yourself will soon outweigh any sacrifice!

Mentors and Seminars

You will need to become an expert in your field. There is a difference between following your passion and *monetizing it!* The fastest way to become an expert is to find mentors who have experience in your chosen field or industry. A mentor should be seasoned. Not only should they be successful in their field, but they should know about many of the mistakes you need to avoid. You can learn what to do and what not to do by tapping into the experience of someone who has already done what you want to do. This will save you an enormous amount of time and money since you can benefit from their mistakes.

The fastest way to become educated in a new industry is to attend seminars. This is exactly how I went from a shy guy in IT to becoming a real estate investor; little did I know it would lead to a career as a professional speaker. I knew that I would need to learn sales skills and how to make public presentations. The fastest way for me to learn these skills was to take a seminar.

If you have the time, you can go back to school. Most people don't have the time or money for schooling. By searching on the internet, you can find seminars or boot camps that focus solely on your passion. The people hosting the seminars typically cram as much information as they can into that event and offer additional information in the form of books, audio and video programs, and training manuals to take home. You might even talk one of the instructors into becoming a mentor for you - just as I did. Your goal is to find a few golden nuggets at each event you attend. The more nuggets you can learn, the faster you will become an expert.

From Part-time Start Up to a Successful System

Test your ideas before making big changes. Start your business part time. This will allow you to build your business without the pressure of having to generate an income right away. You'll also have time to build relationships with customers and suppliers. You'll see how your business plan is working and discover if you need to modify it to meet your customer's needs. I was able to grow my speaking business by speaking once a month at events. I quickly learned about the speaking industry and got to interact with other speakers.

Every successful business has systems in place that allow them to be profitable right from the start. Does McDonald's make the best hamburgers? No! Yet, they are a very successful business; in 2009 they served more than fifty-eight million hamburgers each day! Why are they successful? Every McDonald's franchise follows the same system. This has allowed them to duplicate the "McDonald's Experience" all around the world.

Your job as the boss and creator of your business will require you to focus on growing it and not getting stuck in the day-to-day operations of it. Your business may start out with just one employee, but as it grows, you will need to outsource work or hire employees to keep up with your company's growth. You will be able to bring new workers up to speed quickly if you have a system in place. Then, you just plug them into your system. Every four to six months you will need to review your system to make sure it is still running efficiently and effectively.

Website and Marketing

Thanks to the Internet, you no longer need a "brick and mortar" building to run a business. This means that to be successful, you will need to have a significant web presence. If your website looks professional, people will assume *you* are professional...and that includes your e-mail, too!

You don't want to have an AOL, gmail or yahoo email address. When someone has a generic email account, business professionals and potential clients may assume that you are not serious about your business. They may consider that if you are not willing to invest the small amount of money that it takes to get a corporate address for your website, then what else will you skimp on?

Stay on top of all of the social networking sites; doing so will greatly reduce your advertising expenses. Building lists of friends and followers is free. Start building your list today. When something significant happens in your life or business, post it on these sites. This top-of-the-mind awareness will make people more likely to use your business or products when the need arises.

I love having the opportunity to help others on their road to financial freedom. If you ever have a day when you are down, have doubts about your choices, or are just procrastinating, send me an email at **KickMe@hughzaretsky.com** and I will give you a motivational "kick" to get you back on track!

Lauren Bloom is an attorney and internationally-recognized expert in business and professional ethics. She writes for TheStreet.com, the premier online destination for all areas where money and life intersect.

Lauren is the author of the award-winning book *The Art of the Apology – How to Apologize Effectively to Practically Anyone*, and the e-book, *Elegant Ethical Solutions – A Practical Guide to Resolving Dilemmas While Preserving Your Business Relationships.* The *Online MBA Guide* has recognized her blog as one of the fifty best business ethics blogs.

Lauren's expertise comes from more than fourteen years of teaching professionals to responsibly reduce their litigation risk by meeting high ethical standards. To contact Lauren for speaking or consulting services, visit her at:

Websites: *businessethicsspeaker.com*
www.artoftheapology.com
Email: *Lauren@BusinessEthicsSpeaker.com*
LinkedIn: *laurenbloom*
Phone: *703-585-0651*

Chapter Seventeen

I Didn't Get Sued on Purpose!

Lauren M. Bloom

Five Steps You Can Take to Help Keep Your Business Out of Court

If you own your own business or professional firm, the last thing you want to worry about is getting sued. Unfortunately, you may not have a choice. According to the Institute for Legal Reform, the U.S. spent more than $252 billion on litigation in 2008 alone. The odds are good that at some point in the future, you and your company may face the threat of a lawsuit.

Litigation is incredibly expensive, especially if you're the defendant. Even if you ultimately win, the cost of defending your company can put you out of business. Being sued also takes a tremendous emotional toll and distracts you from growing and managing your business.

That's the bad news. The good news is that you can do something about it. Yes, there's always the freak complaint that makes headlines, but most lawsuits come from a few sources and involve fairly predictable issues. *Don't rely on this chapter as a substitute for personalized legal advice.* But recognize that, if you act with purpose, you *can* significantly reduce the risk that you and your firm will have to defend yourselves in court.

Who files business lawsuits?

Here are the people who may be most likely to sue you and your business:

- Unhappy clients or customers
- Your employees
- Your suppliers (including your landlord, contractors and investors)
- Regulators with responsibility to oversee your operations

While there are many accusations a plaintiff's lawyer can make, they usually come down to these basic concepts:

- You didn't keep a promise
- You provided flawed goods or services
- You didn't keep your premises safe
- You didn't warn the plaintiff about a possible bad outcome
- You violated a law that applies to your company

Sounds simple, doesn't it? That's because it often is. Many lawsuits could be prevented if business owners took purposeful steps to manage their litigation risk. Here are some ways that you, as a business owner or entrepreneur, can limit your liability.

1. Promise only what you can deliver

Business promises take many forms: advertising, contracts, employment agreements, codes of ethics, etc. In any competitive business (and what business isn't?) it can be tempting to promise too much, take on more than you can handle, exaggerate what your product can do, or promise more than you can give to that wunderkind employee. *Don't do it!* The law will hold you to your promises, and failing to keep them can cost you big in court. Trust the quality of your goods and services and describe them accurately. Keep your promises. Most important, *never lie* ... not to your customers, your employees, your suppliers, or anybody else!

2. Put it in writing

Whenever you deal with a supplier or regulator, and often with a client, customer or employee, use a written contract. Why? First, because coming to agreement on the contract will flush out any misunderstandings between you and the other person about who's going to do what, when, and how much it's going to cost. Second, a written agreement helps you move ahead with confidence and purpose, because you know what's expected of you. Contracts don't have to be long, complicated documents – often, a page or two is enough to describe everyone's expectations.

Once you have a contract you must, of course, fulfill it. And don't think you have no contract just because there's nothing in writing. You can still be bound by an oral agreement, but it's harder to prove who promised what to whom. That's all the more reason to write it down – proving such things in court can cost a fortune.

It's also smart to put instructions and warnings in writing. That way, if something goes wrong you can show that you told your client, customer, or employee to follow safety directions, or that you couldn't guarantee a particular outcome from the use of a product or service you provided. Otherwise, it's your word against theirs about what you told them, which can generate bad results in court.

3. Do what you can, not just what you must

Your business should satisfy all applicable laws, but it's a mistake to think bare compliance is all you need. The law is a floor, not a ceiling – you can get punished for falling below it, but nothing prevents you from soaring above it. Set high standards of honesty, competence, caring, and quality for every aspect of your business, then strive to meet those standards daily. Keep your premises healthy and safe for customers and employees. Provide the highest quality of goods and services that you can. If you succeed in bringing outstanding ethics to your company, the law will (mostly) take care of itself.

That said, you still need to know what the law requires to avoid pitfalls. Invest in good advice from an attorney who knows your industry, and keep up with changes in the law. You can't comply if you don't know what's required, and ignorance of the law is no excuse for non-compliance.

4. Purposefully investigate and resolve problems

If you've got a problem that could land your company in court, chances are you already know about it. Maybe it's that angry customer whose call you've been avoiding, the vendor who's still waiting to get paid, the salesclerk who's been aggressively romancing the reluctant bookkeeper, or that loose runner on the stairs you never got around to fixing. You tell yourself you have higher priorities, and keep putting it off for a tomorrow that never comes. Bad, bad idea.

Your mother was right – problems never go away just because you ignore them. But the opportunity to resolve a problem out of court can vanish pretty quickly. If you have a problem that could lead to a lawsuit, *act with purpose*: confirm what's wrong, then fix it.

Sometimes, you'll find that someone in your company has made a mistake and that you need to apologize to an angry customer, client, vendor, employee, or regulator. An effective apology can prevent a lawsuit, but making an effective apology takes time, thought and care. In my book, ***The Art of the Apology – How to Apologize Effectively to Practically Anyone*** (available on Amazon or at **www.businessethicsspeaker.com**), I share tips on how to make an apology that can strengthen relationships, restore trust, and keep you and your company out of court.

5. Put relationships first

Forget everything you've heard about sidelining personal relationships in business because, when it comes to litigation risk management, relationships are critical. The medical profession is years ahead of the business world in researching why people sue. The research shows that patients generally don't bring malpractice suits to make millions. They sue because they don't know what happened when a medical procedure went wrong and think they can't find out any other way, or because they think the health care provider didn't care about them. Doctors who have good relationships with their patients, whose patients see them as caring professionals who do their best to serve with honesty and competence, and who keep their patients fully informed, are much less likely to be sued if something goes wrong.

The same holds true in business. If your customers, clients, suppliers, and employees think you care about them and are honest and trustworthy, they'll be inclined to forgive you when mistakes inevitably happen. On the other hand, if they see you as arrogant, dishonest or uncaring, they'll be much more likely to sue you first and ask questions later.

If you wait until you're sued to focus on your business relationships, you're too late. Take the time *now* to develop trust and rapport with your customers and clients, employees, suppliers, and any regulators who happen to drop by. Don't view others as nothing more than an expense, an annoyance, or a source of short-term income. Treat them as singular individuals with needs you can't wait to meet and problems you're eager to solve. You'll prosper, and your company's litigation risk will almost certainly decline.

Conclusion

If all of this sounds like too much trouble, think back to why you went into business in the first place. Did you want to do the work, or spend all your time second-guessing yourself and justifying mistakes, oversights and bad decisions while spending hundreds of dollars an hour to do so? The steps described here can reduce your company's litigation risk and, at the same time, let you focus on bringing your business to the height of success. Act with purpose – the lawsuit you prevent may be your own.

Sharmen Lane, *"The HOW GAL,"* was a high school drop-out/manicurist who became a millionaire as a top sales rep at a multimillion dollar organization. Shar has been highly recognized for her award-winning career in sales.

Today, she shares her experience as a highly-recommended motivational speaker and author. She not only gives her audiences the "WOW," but also the "HOW" to achieving their goals and creating the life they want.

Sharmen has been interviewed on **Lifetime TV**, **NPR, the New York Daily News,** and **BusinessWeek**. She is the host of **Now to Wow** on 96.7 WBLQ. Shar's client list includes Lia Sophia, Isagenix, and World Financial Group, as well as many of the top women's expos in the country. For more information or for a FREE, 15-minute consultation, visit:

Website:	*www.sharspeaks.com*
E-mail:	*shar@sharspeaks.com*
LinkedIn:	*sharmenlane*
Twitter:	*@sharspeaks*
Facebook:	*sharmenlane*
Phone:	*888-582-0582*

Chapter Eighteen

Taking You from Now to WOW!

Sharmen Lane

Have you ever wondered how you got to where you are? Does it sometimes seem as if you magically appeared there, with little or no recollection of the journey? Perhaps you remember the journey, but it is one that you would prefer to forget. Either way, you find yourself in one place, wanting to be in another, and wondering how to get there. You want your life to have more abundance, magic, fulfillment... more "WOW"! Whatever "WOW" means to you, I can help you go *"From Now to WOW!"*

I have found that there are six simple steps to creating the life you want. Identify where you are, realize you always have a choice, be clear about what you want, make a plan to make it happen, take action, and overcome fear.

YOU ARE HERE

It doesn't matter *how* you got to where you are today, or why you're here. "Here" is this moment, where you are right now. Look at where you are from a place without judgment, without opinion. The purpose of examining this moment is simply to know where you are so you have a beginning, a place to start from. You need to be clear about where "here" is. It's just like looking at a map in an amusement park or shopping mall. The map shows a big red arrow pointing at the place in which you are standing that reads, "You Are Here." That's all. No judgment, no criticism, no opinion, just the words, "You Are Here". You can't get to where you want to go if you don't know where you are! This is your "Now," and now that you know where you are, you can begin.

Now, let's take this one step further. Write down the details of where you are. This should include:

- Your current financial situation.

- Your level of education.

- Your romantic status or family life.

- Your job or career.

- Or any other *significant* part of your life.

Write down where you are *in every aspect of your life*. Be clear and honest, without judgment. If you have thirteen cents in your bank account, write that down. If you are thirty or even a hundred pounds overweight, write that down. If you are in a tiny, dark apartment, living paycheck to paycheck, write that down. It can be challenging to do this without judgment, but do it anyway. You have to know where you are starting from, whether you like where you are or not.

CHOICES CHANGE YOUR WORLD

The second step is one of realization. One of the most powerful things that you can do to create WOW in your life is to realize and accept that you always have a choice. Sometimes your choices are limited. Sometimes you have to choose between something and nothing... yet there is still a choice. If someone holds a gun to your head and says give me your wallet, do you have a choice? Yes, surprisingly, you do. In such a case, your choices are limited and undesirable, but you still have choices. I'm sure you've heard that not making a choice IS making a choice. When you choose to do nothing, that – in and of itself, is a choice.

By realizing and accepting that you always have a choice – even when you choose to do nothing - you empower yourself. You can choose to take action and change your life. If you choose to believe that you are stuck in your situation and that you have no choices, then you have no ability to change your situation. Choose now to be the change in your own life.

SET YOUR GOALS

Now that you know where you are and understand that you have always have a choice, you get to choose your future. Ask yourself deep, thought-provoking questions such as:

- What do I *really* want? Do not be vague or careless here. "I just want to be happy" is not enough.

- What would it take to make me happy? Be specific.

- What would be my ideal job or career?

- What would be the ultimate relationship for me? What would it mean to me?

- Where would I live if I had every city and every home from which to choose?

- Am I happy with my current level of education? If not, what degree would I want to earn and from what school?

You essentially have a blank canvas and you can paint any picture on it that you want.

Knowing what you want is the first step to *getting* what you want. If you don't know where you want to go, how will you get there? You will end up somewhere else. If you don't know what you want, you will end up getting whatever happens to come your way. You may like what you get, but you may not. Is your life a game of chance? Or, is your life, starting now, your choice? Choose now to set your goals and identify the life you want, as well as the things you want to have in it.

MAKE A PLAN

Getting what you want is not as simple as just knowing what you want. Setting a goal is just the beginning. You need to make a plan to achieve your goals. Antoine de Saint-Exupery, the French writer, pilot, and author of "The Little Prince," said, "A goal without a plan is just a wish." I agree! Wishes are weak, but a goal with a plan has power. Give your goals the strength and power to actually make them happen by creating a plan. You would never build a home without a plan. You wouldn't get in your car and start driving to somewhere you've never been without a map, GPS, or directions. A plan is your "How." If you know where you are and where you want to go, your plan – or HOW – is your set of instructions or directions that outlines the steps necessary to get to your destination.

When I was in sales, I knew that about half of what I was working on would actually result in a sale. Therefore, I knew I had to work on twice as many deals in order to earn what I wanted. In other words, if I wanted to close 100 deals, I had to "cold call" on 400 people, half of whom would become potential customers. I knew I could close half of those 200, and thereby achieve my goal. That was my "big plan."

Then I broke my plan down into smaller pieces; I call that dicing. Every day I made a plan to see a certain number of customers and every day I did just that. For six years, I hit my mark, every time. That did not happen by accident.

It happened on purpose – and because I had a plan to get to where I wanted to go.

Another example that most people will relate to is this: Suppose you want to lose ten pounds over the next 30 days. It takes 3,500 calories to gain or lose one pound of fat. Take the number of pounds you want to lose and multiply it by 3,500. In this case, it would be 35,000. Take the 35,000 calories and divide it by 30 (number of days in a month), and you'd come up with 1,166. This means that you would have to eat 1,166 fewer calories per day, burn 1,166 calories more than you eat per day, or eat about 583 calories less and burn and 583 calories more in order to lose those 10 pounds. That's the start of a plan. Breaking a plan into little things you can do every day helps to make your goals seem more attainable.

TAKE ACTION

Step five is to put your plan into action. Write down what you are going to do each and every day and then do it. You may need a support system to help you stay on track. Get a friend, coach, or mentor to help you. Touch base with them weekly or daily, if you need. Let them know what you are doing to move toward your goal. Choose someone who will hold you accountable, someone you can count on. Having an accountability partner can be the difference between reaching your goal or not.

OVERCOMING FEAR

On any journey to accomplishing your goals, fear – at some point – will rear its ugly head. I encourage you to change your perspective on fear.

There are only two types of fear:

- Fear that is real.

- Fear that is fake or imagined.

Real fear is something that could cause you physical harm or death. Fake fear is something that only exists in your head. "Fear of failure" or "fear of rejection" are fake fears. They exist only in your mind. They can grab hold and stop us from taking action. Change your perspective and see fake fear for what it is – a figment of your imagination. Take action and pursue your goals.

I wrote my latest book, ***Giving You the Wow and the How,*** to help you to discover the power in you and create the life you really want. I look forward to sharing with you and helping you live the life of your dreams.

A true American success story, **Carlos Rey** delivers a message of hope through adversity.

When his family business was destroyed in 1992 by Hurricane Andrew, Carlos Rey turned to network marketing, where his life's passion for helping others led him to build one of the largest and most successful organizations in the world.

Carlos believes that helping others is not about any particular service or product, but is more about helping people to achieve what they really want. His commitment is to always be realistic, honest, and specific to guide them to their success.

Carlos has helped tens of thousands of people worldwide overcome the obstacles in their lives to achieve greatness. His unique message and outstanding ability to communicate with individuals at every level has assured him a place amongst the great speakers of today.

Website: www.CarlosRey.com
E-mail: Carlos@CarlosRey.com
Twitter: @carlosrey
Phone: 786.553.1775

Chapter Nineteen

Opportunity's Disguise

Carlos Rey

We are each given many opportunities in our lives, though some of them come in the form of adversity. Time and experience have taught me to embrace such challenges, for they are where the real value in life is created. Once you discover how facing and resolving challenges in your own life can become the stepping stones toward success for you and your family, you too, will come to welcome them and the opportunities they bring.

We all encounter difficult times and challenging events. How we choose to deal with them is what ultimately defines us as individuals. We need to develop a mindset that will help us to grow from our experiences and come away with the understanding of what these adversities truly represent in our lives.

A New Start

My family moved to Miami, Florida from Cuba when I was very young. I remember my parents working several jobs to provide for our family. They finally saved enough money to start their own business – a furniture store. Then, unexpectedly, my father passed away. I took over the business at a very young age and transformed our small, family furniture company into a significant business.

Furniture was all I ever knew; I figured I would be in the furniture business for the rest of my life. My father used to tell me "Son, be careful and don't make the same mistake a lot of people make - they learn a profession or business and they get stuck in it." He also said "Be careful you don't become a 'furniture man.' The fact that you know about furniture doesn't mean you should focus just on that. Other opportunities will come your way and you need to be open to looking at them."

My father had seen others make these mistakes and he wanted more for me. Unfortunately, I had become entrenched in the furniture business and did, indeed, feel "stuck in it." I had fallen victim to the very situation my father had warned me about: I had become a "furniture man."

Tragedy Strikes!

Losing my father at a young age and having to take over the family business was hard. Sometimes, when you think nothing worse can happen, circumstances challenge you even more. In 1992, Hurricane Andrew wiped us out. Our hard-earned family business was gone in an instant! It was utterly devastating. In the midst of this disaster, I could not have imagined the personal growth or happiness that would come from such an event. However, if it had not been for this tragedy, my life would not be what it is today.

It took a hurricane's wrath and my father's advice to help me realize that there must be something more for me in life than the furniture business. Through hard work and personal development, including the understanding and implementation of certain principles, I have been able to reach dreams far greater than I ever thought possible.

Challenges represent life's way of teaching you the skills you will need to possess if you are to become successful. These obstacles are just some of what I've had to overcome in my life. I learned early on that it's best to embrace such challenges because they always have a benefit in the end. However, they only represent opportunities for growth IF you are willing to work through them. Such challenges and adversities not only give you the opportunity to build your character, but they also provide you with a blueprint for success the next time a similar situation occurs.

Additionally, as a leader, mentor, or friend - challenges prepare you to better relate to those around you when they experience a similar adversity. You will truly know what they are going through and have a greater understanding of their situation.

I have been through many challenges in my life, both personal and professional. How could

I stand before audiences in my seminars and teach others how to overcome challenges if I have not experienced my own adversities? I am able to come from a place of honesty and first-hand experience. One of my clients, Angela, wrote to me to say that it was easy for her to relate to me because I was able to share some of the more dire circumstances of my own life. Adversity had given us a common bond.

Pulling Away from the Pack

In order for you to overcome challenges, you need to get to a point in your life where you say, "Enough is enough. I'm tired of seeing others become successful while I remain stuck. I've tried to succeed many times in the past but I haven't yet gotten results that make me feel successful. I am now willing to make the necessary changes so that I too, can succeed."

The first step in achieving success is to fan the flames of your desire. If what you've done in the past hasn't worked for you, you need to be willing to do something different. Only then, when you make those changes, will you be able to realize the success you desire. If you are not willing to make these changes, it doesn't matter how many books you read or CDs you listen to. The key is to recognize the changes you need to make and then apply them in your life.

Don't Let Setbacks Hold You Back

Take notice of your setbacks and make adjustments so that you can avoid them in the future. Too many people say, "I tried that once; it didn't work." They give up completely rather than trying a new way of doing something. Successful people don't let past failures hold them back. Let each challenge remind you of why you are moving in a certain direction. Let it reinforce your positive, non-compromising efforts to ensure your success.

Attitudes and Habits

In your journey toward success, you must develop and maintain a positive mental attitude and form positive habits that will support your goals. These three simple habits have allowed me to build one of the largest organizations in the history of network marketing. I credit them with sending me to top of two major network marketing companies in record time.

1. **Start your day very early.** By giving myself an extra thirty minutes at the start of each day, which I spend reading or listening to positive personal development programs, I am better prepared for the challenges of the day. We have to reprogram our minds to dismiss the negative thoughts and foster the positive ones. Interestingly enough, in my many years of teaching personal development, I've never met a negative person who thinks they are negative! It

takes a constant effort at first to hold only positive thoughts in your mind.

2. **Get into the habit of under-promising and over-delivering.** Your words are very powerful. People will remember what you say and hold you accountable for your actions.

3. **Have a written plan for your success that is specific, measurable, and attainable.** This will allow you to set higher and higher goals as simpler goals are achieved. This also gives you a track record of success that will boost your self-confidence by knowing that you regularly achieve the goals you set for yourself.

Take Responsibility

True leaders take responsibility for occurrences in their lives - both good and bad. Every morning I thank God for the challenges of yesterday. I search for the lessons in everything that happens. I also ask myself a very important question; "How can I improve so that I can have better results next time?" Most people tend to see themselves as victims. They blame their circumstances, the economy, or their friends or family for everything that goes wrong in their lives.

Unsuccessful people think about their problems and challenges and just hope everything will work out. A leader will jump right into the solution. In retrospect, it's easy to see how many of the challenges that I have had to work through turned into some of the greatest blessings in my life.

Feelings vs. Success

Feelings have nothing to do with behavior or becoming successful. Most people let their feelings dictate their behavior. When people say things like, "I don't feel like doing this now," or "I'll get around to it when I feel like it," it is a clear indication that they are letting their feelings drive their success (or lack of it!) Successful people, however, are in the habit of doing things **NOW** – no matter how miniscule the task. If you practice this simple principle for the next thirty days in a row, (the time it takes to enforce a new habit), you'll be surprised at how your life will begin to change for the better.

The law of attraction is real and very powerful. By changing your habits and attitude, taking responsibility, and taking action, you will start to attract more positive people who will want to be around you and take part in what you are doing. Drawing from my life experiences as well as those of others, I have been fortunate enough to have helped many people through their challenges, by taking them by the hand and, step by step, showing them how to overcome their challenges. Success lies in being able to recognize the opportunities that each new day holds for us.

Robin Jay is in demand as a Business Relationship Expert who shares the nuts-and-bolts of building *profitable business relationships.*

Her clients affectionately nicknamed her the *"The Queen of the Business Lunch,"* which led her to write her award-winning signature book, ***The Art of the Business Lunch***, now in twelve languages. Her newest work, ***B Face 2 Face 4 Success***, brings essential elements – including social media and technology – into the business relationship mix to help professionals build their most committed, productive, and profitable relationships ever.

Robin has been featured internationally on ***MSNBC-TV, Newsweek, the BBC, CNN, Forbes. com, The New York Times***, and more. For more information on Robin, please visit:

>   *Website: www.RobinJay.com*
>   *E-mail: Robin@RobinJay.com*
>   *LinkedIn: RobinJay*
>   *Twitter: @lunchwriter*
>   *Facebook: RobinJay*
>   *Phone: 702-460-1420*

Chapter Twenty

B Face 2 Face 4 Success!

Robin Jay

Bob Dylan summed it up when he sang, "The times they are a-changing." The very technology that was designed to make our lives easier has consumed us instead. We barely have time to write complete sentences anymore! We have never before had so much to do and so little time in which to do it!

In spite of all the changes in business lately, the bottom line remains the same: *"People prefer to do business with people they like."* Generating quality one-on-one **"face time"** is still the best way to build relationships, in business and in life. Now, we can use technology as a tool for acquiring more face time, and then use that time to become even more productive and profitable.

We need to do all we can to build solid, mutually-beneficial relationships. Just as the 3-martini **"Power Lunch"** of the 1960's is long gone, so are the languishing lunches in which I used to indulge. I have other events on my schedule, as do my clients. We have meetings, appointments, and pressing work, so business lunches are more efficient now. Doing a business lunch effectively takes focus, preparedness, and energy. Client lunches are more valuable than ever for creating quality face time, breaking down barriers, and finding common ground. Take your clients out to lunch whenever you can; business lunches are a great way to stimulate your business and the economy. Nobody wins when you eat at your desk. In today's business world, a great business lunch is merely the meat in a bigger enchilada.

Adapt to New Technology

Building strong relationships is vital to your success. Adaptability is key. Take advantage of new technology and use it to strengthen your existing relationships, reach out to new people in distant locations, and develop more committed, trusting relationships.

Today, we **"txt msg."** We also send 140 character **Tweets** on **Twitter** to share our vital (and viral) messages. We post status updates on **Facebook** for all our contacts to see. Text messaging became a cheap way to say, "Hi" or "I'm running late" back when cell calls were expensive. Now, people are hooked. You can even text a Tweet!

Text messaging is popular because it is quiet; you can text when you are supposed to be doing something else – from sharing quality time with your family to paying attention in meetings or seminars. Professional speakers and meeting leaders really need to captivate and entertain if they expect their audiences to put away their phones and pay attention! Also, it's never okay to send or read messages when out with clients – even if you think you are being discreet while doing so!

Make Time for Face Time

With all these text messages, Tweets, and Facebook updates, what happens to the all-important FACE TIME? Is it as important as before? The answer is YES! Staying on the cutting edge of technology is critical, but *relationships* are what drive dollars and deals. **WHO you know is still as important as WHAT you know.** That is why it's more essential than ever to *make time for face time* with your clients... then use it to find out how you can help them do a better job at *their* job.

In spite of trimmed budgets, the successful business owners I know are still taking their clients out; they play golf for hours, then relax at the "19th hole" over a beer; they take their clients to boxing matches and concerts; they invite clients and their families to join them for picnics, sporting events, or a day at the lake. I was talking with my friend Phil about socializing with clients. Phil said, "You know... thinking about it, I realize that **I have NEVER lost a client** who has been to my home for dinner." The proof, as they say, is in the pudding.

Initiating and Cultivating Relationships

Networking is still one of the most effective ways to meet new contacts, stay in touch, and build your business and social circles. Use technology to generate industry and colleague **Meet Ups** for the perfect mix of high-tech and high-touch.

To make sure you are getting the best ROI (return on investment) for your networking and socializing dollars, you need to *authenticate* where your dollars are going to be spent. If your socializing budget is just $100 - $200 a month, determine *ahead of time* how to spend that to your utmost advantage. Your plan for the month might include a chamber of commerce breakfast, three morning coffee meetings, two lunches, and one cocktail mixer. $200 can go a long way toward gaining quality face time when you plan how to spend it effectively.

While networking is essential to meeting people and building new relationships, be sure not to neglect your existing clients. "Outta sight, outta mind" is as true in business as it is in personal relationships. Make sure that you are in front of your clients as often as possible. Remember, your competition is just waiting for you to get too busy generating new business so that they can swoop in and scoop up your clients and their business! Stop by with doughnuts, information, or opportunities, but don't let a month go by without touching base.

Become Your Client's Most Valuable Resource

Pay attention to the world around you – industry news, community events, and more. In my book, *The Art of the Business Lunch*, I shared a story about a client of mine who called me from her hospital bed after open heart surgery. She was looking for the best restaurant near the hospital so her visiting family could grab a bite. It's significant that she knew I would have an answer.

Social media can help you to be in two places at once when you use it to become your client's most valuable resource. Post important information about your industry or your community on Facebook and Twitter, and **write a blog** so that your clients will come to count on you for the latest updates, trends, and information. Encourage them to subscribe to your blog so they will get your updates automatically. Then, make it worth their while by delivering essential information they can use. You'll create top-of-the-mind awareness while quickly becoming your client's most valuable resource, which will mean more business for you in the long run.

When You Can't Be There

Sometimes, we don't have the luxury of enjoying quality face time. In building global business relationships, we can still achieve our goals; we simply need to become more creative. Through creativity, I have built amazing relationships with people from all over the world.

The internet, Skype, and computer cameras enable us to look at the people we are talking to in "real time." It's incredible. **LinkedIn** is also tremendous for initiating and developing long-distance relationships. Their **"recommendations"** feature is critical in helping to define yourself as an expert in your field. It can instill confidence in those you want to get to know or those who want to know you, much as "feedback" does for buyers on Ebay. Take the time to recommend others and ask for recommendations in return.

You can improve your connection with long-distance clients by discovering common ground. Is there something you can send them – a book, a trinket, a high-tech toy – that would let them know how much you value your relationship with them? Betty, an event planner, heard me speak at a Meeting Professionals International event and we've stayed in touch ever since. We discovered we are both "dog people." I sent her a "Talking Bone" that allowed me to record a greeting for her dogs. "Hi, Paco... Hi Reina... How are you? It's Robin and Georgie! (my dog) Hope you like your new bone!" Betty AND her dogs loved the gift. She said she hears my voice *all day long!* It's not about sending expensive gifts; it's simply a matter of being thoughtful and creative in coming up with a perfect gift or other unique way of staying in touch that will show your client how much you care.

The New Buzzword: Transparency

One of the most important benefits that quality face time will afford you is the opportunity to share something that has become essential to business success today: trust, openness, transparency... call it what you will. We live in a time of caution. People WANT to believe you are good, but your words, thoughts, and deeds are what will *prove* that you deserve their trust. It's harder to build trust with e-mails and phone calls, and darn near impossible to build trust with text messages.

As a writer, I have found that I'm able to share openly with others through my writing. I know this because people comment on it. When we finally get to meet each other, the groundwork for a trusting relationship has been laid. But there is no substitute for looking someone in the eye, telling them you'll be there for them, and then proving it through your actions. That is a key for success in business and in life.

Take advantage of new technology, devices, and services to help you in business, and remember that there is no substitute for quality face time when it comes to building strong relationships. Staying up-to-date on technology, getting clear on your relationship goals, sharing openly and honestly, and incorporating these characteristics into quality face time will propel you to the pinnacle of success. Make the time and effort to see and be seen. Build relationships and achieve your goals: B Face 2 Face 4 Success!

NOTES

The Power of the Platform
Speakers on Purpose

If you would like to order additional copies of
The Power of the Platform: *Speakers on Purpose*
please visit www.LVCSB.com
or call 702-460-1420.

*Special discounts are available on orders of fifty
books or more.*

The Las Vegas Convention Speakers Bureau
www.LVCSB.com

Are you a speaker? For information on becoming
published in an upcoming edition of
The Power of the Platform,
please contact us immediately.
E-mail: *Robin@LVCSB.com*
or call 702-460-1420.

Engage your passion ~ Find your purpose!
Do what you love, help others, and make money!

*The Las Vegas Convention Speakers Bureau
offers coaching on speaking, writing, publishing,
and marketing. Our team of experts will help you
to achieve your speaking and publishing goals.*

The Las Vegas Convention Speakers Bureau provides professional keynote, motivational, and inspirational speakers as well as outstanding entertainers for conventions, conferences, seminars, and meetings.

Whether you need a speaker to improve your company's attitude, to boost productivity and sales, or to share the latest insights on networking, leadership, communication, customer service, humor, management, branding, building relationships, overcoming adversity, business ethics, diversity, or any other topic, the Las Vegas Convention Speakers Bureau has just the right speaker to make your meeting the most memorable, ever!

We will work with you one-on-one to determine your special needs, then recommend only the finest, most appropriate, and engaging speakers or entertainers – each of whom will work passionately to deliver impact to your event.

For a presentation that will be the highlight of your event, please call or e-mail us immediately! We look forward to working with you to create an event that will net high scores for your keynotes, breakouts, and general sessions and rave reviews for you!

**For a FREE E-book
Visit: www.LVCSB.com/FreeEbook/**

LAS VEGAS
CONVENTION
SPEAKERS BUREAU

~ Featuring World-Class Speakers,
Entertainers & Athletes
Robin@LVCSB.com
www.LVCSB.com
702-460-1420